WHITE HOUSE CALL GIRL

FERAL HOUSE

WHITE HOUSE CALL GIRL

THE REAL WATERGATE STORY

BY PHIL STANFORD

Feral House

1240 W. Sims Way Suite 124

Port Townsend, WA 98368

design by designSimple

For my brothers, Jim and Ron, who read it here first.

Contents

Roy H. Roth
DETROIT   BEVERLY HILLS,
MICH.   CALIF.

HEIDI

Foreword

Heidi's the name. And in case you haven't figured out the game yet, you might want to take a peek at one of her earlier nude photos, circa 1957 or 58—which is to say, roughly fifteen years before she either did or didn't get involved in the Watergate affair.

That, of course, is the question before us.

It's how she got her start, you see—moonlighting as a nude model while still serving as a private in the U.S. Army in Washington, D.C. Not long after she arrived at her duty station in the nation's capital, she was named "Miss Fort Myer." The photographer who covered the event asked her if she'd like to do something a little more interesting, and as so often happens, one thing led to another.

And while that may not be a typical career path for an aspiring photographer's model—or stripper, which was Heidi's next big career move—you can see how it might have worked for her.

So if the soft curves and round, plump nipples offend your sense of historical propriety, just take a deep breath and think of it as documentary evidence—because that's what it is. If you didn't know before what it takes to get into the jet set party girl business, well, now you've got a pretty good idea.

More importantly, though, the photo should lend some flesh and blood substance to the life of a woman whose ghost has hovered over the Watergate saga for years now. Even today, as we go about celebrating the fortieth anniversary of that long-ago political scandal, there is a nasty little argument among Watergate scholars, not to mention all the others who have axes to grind, over what role, if any, she played.

As it happens, there's a good deal of evidence that a call girl operation Heidi was running in 1972 triggered the infamous break-in that led to the downfall of the thirty-seventh president of the United States, Richard M. Nixon.

Needless to say, this is not part of the Watergate story that has come down to us over the decades. There are, in fact, those who disagree so vehemently with this version of events that they've sued—unsuccessfully, as it's turned out—to prevent it from being discussed in print.

It is also only fair to point out that virtually all the more conventional Watergate histories—but especially the more-or-less official version as propounded by the *Washington Post*—dismiss it out of hand as dangerous "revisionist" history.[1] If you're not careful, you might even end up being called a "conspiracy theorist."

And if all else fails, they can always call you crazy—which is what happened to a young lawyer named Phillip Bailey, one of the principal witnesses to this roundly ignored bit of American history. When it appeared that he might be foolish enough to blow the whistle on Heidi and her call girl ring, he was locked up at St. Elizabeth's, the District of Columbia's mental hospital. In the ward for the criminally insane, no less.

Some forty years later, rhetorically at least, that's still the last line of defense for those who would like this story to go away.

Well, at least you can't say you haven't been warned.

GOP Security Aide Among 5 Arrested In Bugging Affair

By Bob Woodward and Carl Bernstein
Washington Post Staff Writers

One of the five men arrested early Saturday in the attempt to bug the Democratic National Committee headquarters here is the salaried security coordinator for Nixon's re-

Dole issued a similar statement, adding that "we deplore action of this kind in or out of politics." An aide to Dole said he was unsure at this time exactly what security services McCord was hired to perform by the

5 Held in Plot to Bug Democrats' Office Here

By Alfred E. Lewis
Washington Post Staff Writer

Five men, one of whom said he is a former employee of the Central Intelligence Agency, were arrested at 2:30 a.m. yesterday in what authorities described as an

elaborate plot to bug the offices of the Democratic National Committee here.

Three of the men were native-born Cubans and another was said to have trained Cuban exiles for guer-

rilla activity after the 1961 Bay of Pigs invasion.

They were surprised at gunpoint by three plain-clothes officers of the metropolitan police department in a sixth-floor office at the plush Watergate, 2600 Virginia Ave.

hite House Consultant Tied to Bug

Bob Woodward
E. J. Bachinski
ton Post Staff Writers

sultant to White
cial counsel Charles
is listed in the ad-
ks of two of the five

In addition, a stamped, un-
mailed envelope containing
Hunt's personal check for $6
made out to the Lakewood
Country Club in Rockville,
and a bill for the same amount
also were found among the sus-

CIA. The other three are either active in the anti-Castro
movement in Florida or are
known by leaders of that
movement

In other developments yesterday:

• It was reported that one
of the five suspects. Eugenio

Jr., a suspect who
for the Republicans as
rity coordinator, served
four months ago in a
15-member military
unit. The Washington
unit develops lists of r
and draws up conti
plans for censorship

Headlines from the Washington Post, *summer of 1973.*

Five Men in Suits

It's two thirty a.m. on a sweaty summer night in Washington, D.C., June 17, 1972. Five men in business suits, wearing surgical gloves and carrying electronic and photographic gear, are arrested at gunpoint inside the headquarters of the Democratic National Committee—located, as we will never be allowed to forget, on the sixth floor of a plush new apartment and office complex called the Watergate.

The police quickly trace the burglars to the White House, home and headquarters of Republican President Richard M. Nixon. At first, the White House press secretary tries to brush it off, calling it a "third-rate burglary." But there's obviously something fishy going on here.

Day after day, the newspapers pick apart the cover-up. Before long, what began as a public embarrassment has become a political firestorm. Within the year, the nation is glued to their television sets, watching almost daily installments of the Watergate hearings conducted by a Special Watergate Committee of the U.S. Senate.

Today, some forty years later, "Watergate" is not just the name of a political scandal that resulted in the resignation—the first and only time ever—of a president of the United States. It has passed into the language and become the suffix of choice for scandal itself. Liquor-gate, Contra-gate, Bounty-gate, you name it.

Yet, oddly enough, no one really knows for sure why the burglary took place.

Certainly, there are those who will tell you they do. The standard version, endorsed by the Senate Watergate Committee itself, is that it was to gather political intelligence on the Democrats. Also, that it was undoubtedly ordered by the ranking members—All the President's Men, if you will—of the Nixon administration.

After all, why else would five guys in suits, carrying electronic and photographic gear, with connections to the White House, be poking around in DNC headquarters in the middle of the night? Case closed, right?

For those who subscribe to the conventional line on Watergate, the heroes of this political morality tale are the two young *Washington Post* reporters, Bob Woodward and Carl Bernstein, who, along with their mysterious tipster, Deep Throat, exposed the White House cover-up and ultimately brought down the president.

Right up there with them is the Watergate committee's star witness, John Dean. Who can forget him, horned-rimmed glasses and all, testifying to the packed galleries: the earnest young White House aide who saw the error of his ways in time to step forward and save the Republic.

It's a great story, the stuff that Academy Award-winning movies are made of. The only problem is that it's not entirely true.

From the beginning, there were rumors[2] that the break-in at DNC head-quarters actually had more to do with a nearby call girl operation than it did with political intelligence gathering. Before a judge sealed the evidence[3] of phone conversations that had been overheard at the DNC, the original prose-cutor of the Watergate burglars was apparently going to allege that the break-in was to gather material for sexual blackmail. Over the years, in fact, there's been a steady accumulation of evidence linking the call girl operation to key players in the Watergate drama.

And at the center of this alternative version of Watergate history is a former stripper named Heidi Rikan, said to be running a call girl operation a block or so from the Watergate at another big apartment complex called the Columbia Plaza. According to those who find this theory worth considering, the burglary was most likely committed to obtain blackmail information on clients the DNC was sending to the Columbia Plaza.

The Watergate, a plush, new office and apartment complex.

A Little Black Book

According to the Revisionists, we've even got the good guys and bad guys mixed up. The way they see it, John Dean isn't the hero of Watergate at all. He is, in fact, Watergate's arch villain. Not only did he order the fateful break-in at the DNC offices, but once the burglars were arrested, he directed the White House cover-up.

And then, when it became obvious that the cover-up was going to crumble, Dean switched sides in exchange for a deal and became the star witness for the prosecution.

Precisely what Dean expected to accomplish by sending burglars into the DNC—whether to gather information on some of the call girl ring's clients, who were being referred from the DNC, or to save himself from a possible political sex scandal— remains unclear.

Certainly, Dean admits to no such thing. However, as everyone in the Revisionist camp agrees, if he did in fact order the break-in, it undoubtedly had something to do with the fact that Dean's live-in girlfriend at the time, Maureen, was a close friend and former roommate of Heidi's, as well.

The debate has gone back and forth, with neither side gaining much ground in recent years—at least since a federal court ruling[4] in 2002 declared that it was okay to discuss the subject in public. Otherwise, it's been little more than a matter of name-calling.

The most recent dustup occurred last year, when a new biography[5] of Ben Bradlee, Woodward's editor at the *Washington Post*, quoted Bradlee as saying he always suspected that there was something phony about Woodward's legendary source, Deep Throat. Woodward, who has gone on from Watergate to become an iconic figure in the world of journalism, counter-attacked immediately, accusing the author (a former assistant of his named Jeff Himmelman) of "dishonesty," despite the fact that Himmelman was working from a transcript of an interview with Bradlee.

Clearly, this is still hotly disputed territory. Not just an empire, but reputations and careers were lost and won over Watergate. So it is understandable that some of those who came out on top might not take kindly to anyone attempting to advance a version of the story that doesn't coincide with the one that brought them fame and glory.

But if, in fact, a former stripper named Heidi Rikan was a central figure in the Watergate affair, the least we can do is find out more about her and see if the facts fall in place. Somehow, despite the court cases and all the books that have been written on the subject, that's something that no one on either side of the controversy has bothered to do. As it turns out, there's a great deal of new information out there, including the recollections of a number of Heidi's friends and family who had apparently not been interviewed before.

And that's not all. We've got Heidi's little black book.

Heidi's younger sister, Kathie, found it more than twenty years ago, shortly after Heidi died on January 27, 1990. And while the book doesn't answer all the questions surrounding the Watergate break-in, it does fill in a lot of blanks.

As Kathie recalls, all of Heidi's earthly belongings were stuffed inside five or six cardboard barrels in their mother's basement. Inside the barrels were a few furs and some jewelry. Some photos, of course.

And at the bottom of one of the barrels, there was Heidi's personal phone directory—filled with the names and phone numbers of famous athletes, mobsters, movie stars, bookies, playboy millionaires, and, of course, politicians and government officials of every stripe from the '60s and '70s.

Some of the names Kathie actually recognized, and not just because they'd been plastered all over the news some years before. As a young girl, Kathie always stayed with Heidi over school vacations, so she'd met some of her friends.

One of them was Heidi's close friend Maureen Dean, or Mo as she was also called. Not surprisingly, John Dean's name was in there too. There are, in fact, multiple listings for both of them in Heidi's little black book, as well as addresses and phone numbers for other government officials who figured in the Watergate scandal.

When Kathie discovered it, the little black book was potential dynamite. John and Maureen Dean were in the process of suing a large number of individuals for daring to entertain the notion that they might have had something to do with the Watergate break-in.

In fact, Maureen called Kathie at about this time to warn her that investigators might be poking around, trying to find out about Heidi. Of course, Kathie could have told her about the book then, but she didn't because she had other things on her mind. She was going through a divorce, which required a lot of her energy. Besides, she just didn't want to get involved.

So she took the little black book—there are two of them actually, a large one and a smaller one Heidi apparently used as a backup—and put them in a safe deposit box, and that is where they have remained for the past twenty years. This is also the first time Kathie has spoken about her sister with anyone outside the circle of her family and close friends.

The Riecken family — Heinrich, Edith, grandmother, and Adelheidcharlott.

Adelheidcharlott, PFC

The woman we now know as Heidi Rikan was born October 19, 1937, in Kiel, Germany, as Adelheidcharlott Riecken. Her father, Heinrich, was an enlisted man in the German navy, and during the war, her mother, Edith, worked in one of the torpedo factories located along the northern coast of Germany.

It was, of course, a terrible time. Edith, who died in 2000, told Kathie she was bombed out three times and left with nothing except the suitcase in her hands. Worse, as the war neared its end, the German government, as part of an effort to free up its female workforce to spend more time in the weapons factories, removed Heidi from her home and placed her in a state-run camp.

At the end of the war, Heidi was located and returned to her home by the International Red Cross. Edith recalled that Heidi, who would have been about eight then, came back a changed little girl. She'd sit in the corner for hours, sucking her thumb.

In 1951, the Riecken family—mother, father and fourteen-year-old Heidi—immigrated to the United States. After spending some time in the lower grades learning English, Heidi attended high school in Reading, Pennsylvania. She graduated in the spring of 1956. The year 1956 was a momentous one for the family in several other ways as well:

In January, Heidi's mother, Edith, got a divorce from Heinrich Riecken.

In February, she married Carl Meck, a trucker thirteen years younger than herself.

In August, just six months later, Kathie was born, with Edith and Carl Meck named as parents on her birth certificate.

Then in December, Heidi enlisted in the army.

On the face of it, it might appear that Edith had been carrying on an affair with Meck while still married to Heinrich. The actual truth, however, may be much darker. As Edith told Kathie many years later, the "final straw" before the divorce was when she came home from work one day and found Heinrich in bed with Heidi.

In other words, there is a real possibility—one that bedevils Kathie to this day—that Heidi is actually her sister *and* her mother.[6] If this is so, however, no one in the family was ever able to talk about it—least of all Heidi, who from an early age developed a reputation for keeping everything inside.

As Kathie tries to explain, "We were a very German family, and there were some things we just didn't talk about." Obviously, though, that explanation goes only so far.

An article in the *Reading Eagle* catches Heidi, or Adlelheidcharlott as she was still called, home on leave in January 1958. According to the reporter—who, in the newspaper style of the time, saw no reason to hide his admiration for the young private's non–military attributes—Heidi was well on her way to a successful army career.

"The WAC lovely," who, he noted, "shows beautiful streamlined curves even in an Army uniform," had already been chosen Miss Ft. Myer and Miss Military District of Columbia, performed the hula for the Second Army special service unit, and was about to be assigned to a new duty station in Heidelberg, Germany, as an interpreter.

There's no telling what heights his prose might have reached if he'd known about Heidi's sideline as a nude model. And certainly, there's no way he or anyone else—except possibly Heidi and her new boyfriend, army helicopter pilot Loren "Buzzy" Patterson—could have predicted that her once-promising army career would soon be a thing of the past.

Buzzy Patterson, now in his late 70s and living in California, remembers the first time he saw Heidi, walking across the campus at Fort Myer. It was the fall of 1957 and he'd just flown a helicopter up from Fort Benning, Georgia. He was twenty-four at the time, a chief warrant officer and decorated combat veteran of the Korean War. She was twenty, and even in uniform, "Boy, was she ever beautiful."

They didn't get in the sack on the first date, he says. But a few weeks later, he drove up to see her again. And pretty soon, as far as the two of them were concerned, they were madly in love. As he recalls quite clearly, she used to coo sweet things to him in German, then giggle when he didn't understand.

Even then, Buzzy says, Heidi was into nude modeling. On one of his D.C. visits, she asked if he wanted to accompany her on a photo shoot.

"Don't worry," she said, "they don't try anything." He went along, and it was just as she said it would be, but he still felt jealous.

Pretty WAC Going Back to Homeland

Local Girl Is Assigned To Germany

When it comes to Army interpreters, the U.S. Army is really going to be "loaded" when it sends Pfc. Adelheidcharlott Riecken to Germany soon.

The pretty WAC daughter of Mrs. Carl Meck of 343 W Windsor St. and Hendrik Riecken of Sheerlund has proven that she is just as hep to bowling over beauty-contest judges as she is at handling the German language.

The WAC lovely, who shows beautiful streamlined curves even in an Army uniform and was graduated from Gov. Mifflin Joint High School in 1956, has all the assets of a top-notch interpreter, even if she does have trouble getting people to pronounce her long first name.

As for her interpreter assets, this first class private with blonde curls framing a pretty face, is equipped with the main ingredients to be successful in her interpreter's job of meeting people.

Since being stationed at Ft. Myer, Va., for the past nine months, Pvt. Riecken was not only chosen "Miss Ft. Myer" in a beauty contest, but she also was selected as "Miss Military District of Washington D.C."

Adelheidcharlott Riecken a recent Army test in German.
Why did Adelheidcharlott

Reading Eagle, *Jan. 16, 1958.*

The young couple married on September 8, 1958, and shortly afterward, Heidi left the army. At the time, being married was reason enough for a woman to be released from military service. Buzzy, knowing that he would be discharged as part of a general cut-back of U.S. forces then underway, also resigned his commission, and the two were civilians again.

A few months later, Buzzy got a job flying for an oil company and left for Colombia. Heidi returned to her mother's home in Reading. From there, the marriage quickly went south.

Whatever the actual reasons for the break-up may have been, Buzzy was flying helicopters in California when Heidi filed for divorce in 1960. He recalls that he got a call from a D.C. lawyer who said Heidi wanted out of the marriage, so he said, "Sure, why not?"

Buzzy didn't learn till years later that Heidi thought he was dead. The lawyer, who'd obviously been trying to put the moves on Heidi, had told her that he'd died as a result of injuries suffered in a crash. He signed some papers and the divorce became final in January 1960.

By this time, Heidi was already back in D.C., endeavoring to start a new career as a stripper on 14th Street.

Heidi at the Blue Mirror.

Stripping at the Blue Mirror

It may come as a surprise to current residents of the nation's capitol that back in the '60s, before the subway system was installed, 14th Street was considered the city's epicenter of vice and sin.

As the *Washington Post* hastened to assure its readers at the time, the "Strip," as they called it, was relatively sedate—at least by comparison with Baltimore's notorious "Block." There were, however, four striptease clubs—the Merry-Land, the Blue Mirror, the Student Prince, and the Parkside—as well as two belly-dancing establishments between the White House and the Capitol. And on any given night, the article noted[7] with a broad wink, you might find "Senators, U.S. Representatives, bank presidents and other substantial and graying or balding citizens . . . among the spectators."

A publicity photo from the Blue Mirror shows that Heidi was using the name Erica, along with an Americanized version of her surname—Erica "Heidi" Rikan. According to Kathie, Heidi had simply become frustrated with the typical American's inability to pronounce Riecken (*Reeken*), much less her even more formidable given name. In the phone book she would henceforth be listed as E.L. Rikan,[8] with the L standing for Lorelei, which she also picked out of thin air. It would not be the last time that Heidi used an assumed name.

One of Heidi's close friends from those years, Carolyn Rainear, would remember Heidi as a girl who "loved celebrity gossip and read everything in those rags like *The Globe* and *The National Enquirer*—and *repeated* what she read as though she was there and it was *true*. Can you imagine?" said Carolyn.

"And she thought of herself as a Marilyn Monroe. Why else the affectation of that wispy little girl voice telling anyone what she thought they wanted to hear. A lot of men wanted to take care of her."[9]

As the Blue Mirror photo reminds us, Heidi certainly had most of the requisites for success as a striptease dancer. Unfortunately, however, as Carolyn would also recall, "Heidi couldn't sing or dance or even move very gracefully on stage, so she was not hired for very long at any place."

What Heidi did do well, though, was get to know a lot of people. And not just the distinguished public servants referenced in the *Post* article. Strip clubs have always straddled the borderline between the straight life and underworld, and Heidi would always have at least one foot in what was then still called the rackets.

Take Heidi's new friend, Carolyn—longtime mistress of Emmitt Warring, dean of the Washington underworld.[10] Warring, or "Little Man," as he was known on the street, was a former bootlegger who'd served time for income tax evasion. In the early '60s, he was still running the city's "numbers" racket, as the lottery was called before the government took it over and made it legal.

And if Heidi knew Carolyn and "Little Man," then she would have to cross paths with Warring's protégé, Joe Nesline. With Warring in semi-retirement by now, Nesline was top dog in the D.C. crime world. Years later, Heidi's mother, Edith, would remember Heidi telling her that she was dating Joe Nesline,[11] an important man in D.C. She didn't approve because Joe was a gambler and a married man, but what could she do?

It also was during this time, Carolyn recalled, that Heidi met an older gentleman, "a retired railroad man"—Uncle Lucien, as the girls called him—who set Heidi up in a nice apartment, gave her a car, her first fur, and lavished her with books and lingerie.

And so, for the rest of her life, Heidi would usually have a sugar daddy to supply her with life's essentials. Of course, under the rules of the game, she was free to have boyfriends on the side, and they of course would also be expected to give her expensive gifts.

As the girls themselves would probably argue, it shouldn't be considered prostitution since no money has actually exchanged hands. How are they different from any other woman looking for the best deal in a conventional marriage?

Of course, from time to time, someone always crosses over the line. There is an affidavit in the court record from gambling figure David McGowan describing in some detail Heidi's activities as a prostitute in D.C.[12] Heidi's younger sister, Kathie, who used to accompany Heidi on her travels, refers to Heidi as a "high class prostitute." And as Heidi herself would one day tell her maid, she was once a call girl—"a call girl at the White House," no less.[13]

It's easiest, however, to think of them as party girls. Or courtesans, which may be the best of all options. It doesn't pay to get too hung up on definitions. After a while, the lines blur.

And besides, who wants money when you can have a Jag, a condo, trips to fabulous places, and a new fur every year—just for being your cute little self?

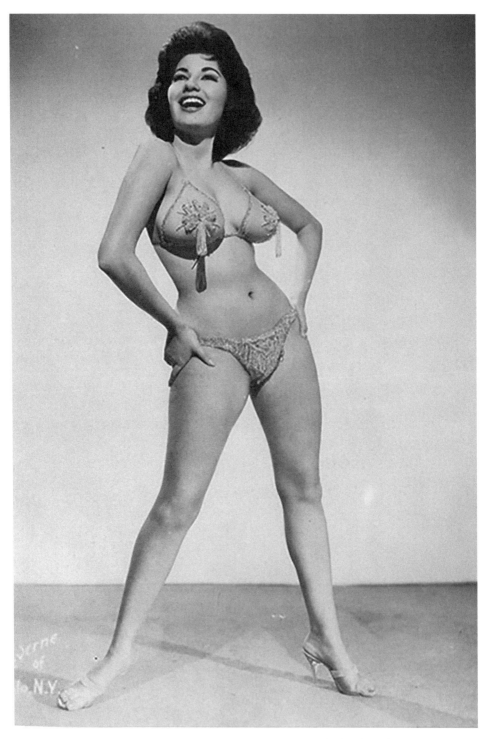

Heidi's friend Josephine Alvarez on stage.

Charlie Was a Nymph

Josephine Alvarez was another of Heidi's new friends. A stripper herself—but good enough to headline at clubs up and down the East Coast—Josephine first met Heidi in 1961. At the time, she was performing at the Merry-Land and Heidi was working a few doors down at the Blue Mirror.

It would be another year or so before their paths would cross again, but it's worth our while to follow her merry adventures in the meantime. As evidenced by her delightfully bawdy autobiography,[14] *Lucky "325,"* Josephine is well worth a book herself. She's also been an extremely valuable source of information, not just on Heidi, whom she came to know quite well, but on the party girl life in general.

Back home in Miami, Josephine was offered an opportunity to travel to the Dominican Republic, along with her girlfriend, Teresita, to entertain the country's dictator, Rafael Trujillo. "Up to that time," writes Josephine, "I had never been involved in an orgy . . . Rafael was very passionate, and the sight of Teresita and I together made his blood race." In payment, she and Teresita received $1,000.

Once Josephine returned to the United States, however, she was offended to learn from her father that the FBI, which had been monitoring their comings and goings, had told him they considered her a prostitute. "'Well,' I said to myself, 'since you have the name *prostitute*, you might as well play the game.'" Whereupon, she bought a ticket to Caracas, Venezuela, and there, shortly after checking into the plush Tamanaco Hotel, met a guest at the hotel pool.

"This relationship went on for weeks. He paid for my hotel bills and gave me money to go shopping. Eventually I had a complete wardrobe. . . . What a wonderful vacation, staying at the best hotel, buying the finest clothes, with spending money generously given me, not to mention wonderful sex with a handsome man."

From there it was back to Miami, first for a torrid affair of several months with another dancer who went by the name Ivory Snow—Josephine is quite open about her bi-sexuality—and then a liaison with an older man who bought her a four-bedroom ocean-front home and a Lincoln Continental convertible.

Unfortunately, however, the older gentleman was arrested for embezzlement, and Josephine was forced to resume her dancing career at the Place Pigalle Club on Miami Beach—where, who should she run run into but Charley "The Blade" Tourine.

Now, it is not for nothing that Tourine, a former mob enforcer, got his nickname. At the time of this encounter with Josephine, however, he had advanced beyond that youthful stage of his career to become one of the top executives in the American criminal world, with business interests including drugs, gambling, and prostitution, up and down the East Coast and abroad.

Tourine, in short, was precisely the sort of older, powerful man that Josephine— who was all of twenty-two at the time—found attractive. Not much later, she moved in with him in his apartment at the Hampshire House on Miami Beach.

"Charlie was a male nymph," she recalls in typically candid fashion. "We had sex six times a day. He was remarkable, with all that stamina at fifty-eight years old, walking around with a perpetual hard-on." In fact, as Josephine goes on to reveal, Charlie was such a good lover she lost several pounds during this time.

Another thing Charlie liked to do, apparently, was cook, and he used to invite his pals over for dinner. Which, as it turns out, is how Josephine's life eventually became entangled with that of Charlie's business partner, Joe Nesline—and through him, once again, with Heidi.

Charley "The Blade" Tourine (top) and Joe Nesline: Mugshots from a 1964 federal gambling bust.

Nesline's the Boss

If Tourine was bad news, so was Nesline. A former street urchin who'd come up the hard way, working as a runner for Emmitt Warring's bootlegging and numbers operations, he was now running the rackets in D.C. He owned three full-service gambling establishments in the D.C. area. One, the Amber Club, located on Southeast Pennsylvania Avenue, catered to the Capitol Hill crowd, as well as high rollers from across the D.C. area.

Nesline had risen to his preeminent position in the D.C. underworld a decade earlier, in 1951, when he shot and killed a man named George Harding in a Georgetown nightspot. Although it was generally believed, at least among his underworld peers, that he did so because Harding had fingered his close friend Warring for a burglary, Nesline's lawyer managed to convince the jury that it was an act of self-defense. But the reputation as a killer stuck.

One of Nesline's greatest assets as a leader of men was, in fact, that he was a little crazy. You never knew when he might go off on you. As the result of a childhood injury, he had a metal plate in his head, and despite all the sedatives and anticonvulsive medications he took to cope with the problem, he was subject to periodic seizures and fits of violence.

As Josephine recalls, she'd actually met Nesline a couple of times on her dancing forays into the Capital City. Nesline had taken her out to dinner once, and although nothing came of it then, she'd been struck by his charming manners and tailored suits, custom made silk shirts, and four-carat green diamond ring with matching cufflinks.

This time, as they sat there in Miami, enjoying Tourine's latest culinary masterpiece, things were different. Nesline, she recalls, gave her an admiring look—"that kind of once-over a man does to a woman." As for Josephine herself, she "couldn't stop staring into those beautiful ice-blue eyes of his."

Even after dinner was over and Joe had returned to his own penthouse apartment—which, as it happened, was located in the Hampshire House just above Tourine's—she couldn't get him out of her mind. "Every time Charlie made love to me," she says, "I was thinking of Joe."

It was, as you've probably guessed already, just a matter of time. One night after dinner was over and Nesline had returned to his penthouse, Josephine faked a phone call and told Tourine that her father needed to see her right away.

Outside, she went to the nearest pay phone and called Nesline, who obligingly told her to come on up, he'd leave the door unlocked.

"That was it for me," writes Josephine. After three days of this—with Tourine calling every so often to ask Nesline if he knew where Josephine might be—Josephine informed the former mob assassin that she could no longer be his sweetheart because her heart belonged to another. As she recalls, Tourine took it pretty well—his exact words being, "Get your fucking shit and get out of my sight."

So Josephine moved in upstairs with Joe. And a few months later, when Joe moved back to D.C. to tend his business interests there, she followed him and checked into a motel. She couldn't move into his house quite yet, she explains, because Joe's wife Gladys was dying of cancer in a nearby hospital, and it just didn't seem right. Instead, says Josephine, she and Nesline would meet every afternoon at her motel and make passionate love before she had to go to work at the Merry-Land.

In D.C., Nesline introduced Josephine to his friend Emmitt Warring and to Warring's longtime mistress Carolyn Rainear– and, of course, Heidi, who was now part of that circle. Although, as she notes in her book, "Heidi had her eye on Joe"—meaning it was pretty obvious Heidi had been having an affair with him—Heidi seemed to accept the fact that "I was the one who had captured his heart . . . and nothing more came of it." Heidi and Josephine soon became close friends.

After Gladys Nesline died in September 1964, Josephine moved into Joe's house in Hyattsville, Maryland. There, she and Heidi would sit around all day playing Scrabble or Monopoly. Josephine would smoke pot and Heidi drank champagne. After a late lunch, maybe they'd stop by the beauty parlor or do a little shopping. Then in the evenings, they'd go out to Billy's, the mob hangout on Vermont Avenue, for dinner and drinks.

As Josephine couldn't help but notice, Heidi, who by this time was no longer stripping, was doing pretty well for someone who had no visible means of support. Of course, Josephine knew about Heidi's sugar daddy—Uncle Lucien—but figured there was no way he could provide some of the luxuries her new best friend now seemed to be enjoying. In addition to some striking pieces of jewelry and a fur coat, Heidi was now driving a Jaguar XKE convertible.

Heidi never talked about it, though. As Josephine would come to realize, Heidi never really talked about anything personal. She was completely close-mouthed. It only made Josephine wonder all the more: Where was Heidi getting that kind of money?

Heidi, Josephine, and Nesline at Billy's.

Hail to the Redskins

Half a century later, it's much easier to see what Heidi was up to. For starters, she was certainly getting to know a lot of professional football players—up close and personal, as they used to say on the sports shows.

And if Josephine couldn't figure it out at the time, it was certainly no mystery to the proprietors of Billy's, Billy Rice and his partner Mae Sullivan. As they would tell a police investigator[15] a few years later, Nesline, who controlled football betting in D.C., was using her to get inside information on football players.

The little black book Heidi was beginning to keep about this time is full of them: Washington Redskins stars Sonny Jurgenson, Billy Kilmer, Diron Talbert, and Eddie Khayat; the Green Bay Packers' Paul Hornung, Donny Anderson, and Max McGee; Dallas's Don Meredith, Craig Morton, and Lance Rentzel—and that's just for starters.[16] And while it would be unfair to suppose that any of the players listed were anything more than innocent targets, their presence in Heidi's book does seem to demonstrate that Heidi was doing a bang-up job.

Over the years, as documented in Dan Moldea's 1989 exposé, *Interference,* organized crime has effectively controlled pro football betting in this country. And if that was true at the time the book was published, it was even more so in the '60s when Heidi was getting started. Sports betting is an enormously lucrative business, because, as with the casinos, the house always wins. Those who run such operations take a ten percent commission on every losing bet—and billions of dollars are bet each year.

In addition, of course, there is always the possibility that someone will try to make an even bigger score by influencing the outcome of a game. It doesn't happen that often—and the NFL denies that it has ever happened at all—but as one veteran sports gambler told Moldea, he was "personally involved in the fixing[17] of no less than thirty-two NFL games" during the '50s and '60s. As Moldea also reported, in the late '60s an IRS investigation[18] into football betting was squelched at the last minute before subpoenas could be delivered to several of the top Redskins players.[19]

As the top dog in D.C.'s multimillion dollar football betting industry, Nesline understood the value of having inside information on injuries or personal problems of star players who would be in a position to influence the outcomes of games. It was useful in setting the betting line, or if Nesline were so inclined, placing a wager of his own now and then.

If Josephine didn't pick up on her friend's role in the football betting industry, however, it didn't take her long to figure out what else Heidi might be doing to keep herself in Jaguars and furs. In the fall of 1964, shortly after Josephine moved in with Nesline, the two of them left for Europe—on what, in retrospect, was clearly much more than a pleasure trip.

Their first stop was London, where Nesline met up with his old friend Dino Cellini, one of Meyer Lansky's closest associates. Just five years before, Nesline and Cellini had worked together at the mob-controlled Tropicana hotel and casino in Havana. Now that the mob was no longer welcome in Castro's Cuba, it was looking to establish new gambling operations—and not just in the Caribbean but in Europe as well. Cellini, along with several other mob figures, was now running a casino in London called the Colony Sport Club, and Nesline was one of his partners.

After a layover in Paris, the couple traveled on to Geneva, Switzerland, where they met Heidi—who, as Josephine remembers, walked off the plane "all dolled up in her beige mink coat, with matching hat." Of course, no one had told Josephine why Heidi should be joining them in Europe, and as always, Josephine didn't ask any questions. It wasn't long, however, before she began to put it all together.

As Josephine, now a tarot instructor and living in southern Florida, puts it: "Geneva? Hel-lo." Heidi, she says, was carrying money for the mob.

"In those days," Josephine says, "no one would think of searching a pretty woman all dressed up like that." As Josephine eventually concluded, Heidi was a courier for both Nesline and Emmitt Warring, Nesline's older partner in crime. It was not just a matter of depositing money in Swiss banks. Back in the United States, where bookies routinely "lay off," or sell, bets to other bookies in order to protect themselves against heavy losses, money had to be moved around all the time. And that being the case, it is hardly surprising that Heidi's own little black book would contain the names and phone numbers of virtually every bookie in D.C., as well as a sampling of gamblers and other mobsters[20] from around the country.

It was, in fact, a perfect job for Heidi. As Josephine had already noticed from their daily soirees, Heidi knew how to keep her mouth shut. She rarely talked about anything personal and never talked about how she made a living. "She was cold," says Josephine. "Nice, but very cold."

From Geneva, the three of them took the train to Rome. En route, Josephine says, Joe told her he wanted to have a threesome with Heidi, so she set it up. She says it was the only time she and Heidi ever had sex. Although Josephine knew that Heidi, like herself, was bisexual, she was never attracted to her, she says.

In Rome, Joe started drinking heavily in the hotel dining room. Perhaps, Josephine says, she should have seen it coming. As an epileptic, Joe wasn't supposed to drink. After Joe went back to their room, she dropped in on Heidi, who had the adjoining room.

As she recalls, she was sitting in Heidi's bathroom, watching her remove her makeup, when all of a sudden Joe was standing beside her, yelling that she was planning to sleep with Heidi again. He punched her and grabbed her by the hair, dragging her into Heidi's bedroom. There he pulled out a penknife and tried to stab her in the back. Josephine tried to dodge, but the knife caught her buttocks, sending blood gushing onto the carpet and the walls.

The sight of the blood apparently brought Joe to his senses, because he left the room then, leaving Heidi to care for Josephine and clean up the mess. After the hotel doctor sewed up the wound, Josephine took two sleeping pills and fell asleep. Josephine says Joe never apologized, and she never brought it up herself. Although she would stay with him for another four years, it was, she says, the beginning of the end of her love for Joe.

Heidi, dressed for the beach.

George Owen.

Heidi Does Dallas

In 1966, Heidi and Josephine, along with Nesline, were on the Caribbean island of Antigua, preparing for the opening of a new casino.

Josephine, of course, was just along for the ride. She'd just returned from London, where, as she reports in her book, she'd fallen madly in love with the Crown Prince Fahd of Saudi Arabia. Their arrangement was that when he wanted to see her again, he'd contact her through Heidi.

Heidi was working. According once again to Mae Sullivan and Billy Rice, the proprietors of Billy's, she was in Antigua as a "bookkeeper"[21] for Nesline. But it was obviously not all work and no play, either, because she was about to meet a fellow named George Owen—bosom buddy of millionaires, mobsters,[22] and famous athletes—and, to use one of the more polite terms available, one of the foremost cocksmen of his time.

The proprietor of the University Club, a popular nightspot in Dallas, Texas, Owen was in Antigua with his good friend Bedford Wynne, part owner of the Dallas Cowboys, to see if they couldn't buy the hotel.

It was raining, and as Owen would describe that first meeting in a 1989 interview[23] with the author Len Colodny, he'd just stepped outside the hotel to go to dinner, wearing a white Palm Beach suit.

"And I saw this girl walking a dog, a little white poodle, and this was the prettiest damn girl you ever saw in your life. Built like a brick shithouse. I said goddamn, man, and I just sat down in the mud.

"I said 'I've never seen a son of a bitch as pretty as you and if you jump on my back, I'll take you around the world barefooted. . . . Come on and I'll buy you dinner.'"

Understandably charmed, Heidi agreed. And as Owen summed it up, they went to dinner, drank some wine, had a good time. And since he was going back to Dallas the next day, Heidi came with him.

Owen did have a way with the ladies. One of his earlier girlfriends was the famous stripper and porn star, Candy Barr.[24] In fact, in 1957 when the Dallas police set her up for a marijuana bust, Owen was in her apartment at the time of the arrest. It's unclear whether he was part of the set-up or just in the wrong place at the right time.

Another busty blonde in Owen's life was the singer Diane Wisdom. He was, in fact, still married to her when he hooked up with Heidi in Antigua. As Wisdom explained in a recent interview, she was off touring with Frank Sinatra at the time, and although both she and Owen considered the marriage a thing of the past, neither of them had bothered to do the paperwork.

Back in Dallas, as Owen would later describe it, he and Heidi "got to dating around." Once, he took her to the opening of the Sahara in Tahoe, where the comedienne Phyllis Diller was on stage. "And when we walked in, and Heidi had one of those big fur coats on, and Phyllis Diller saw her, she says, 'Holy Gee. She's too pretty. I hate anybody that pretty.' And so we had a great time, you know."

Through Owen, Heidi would soon meet the movers and shakers[25] of Texas politics—and at a time when they wielded extraordinary influence over the entire nation because their boy, Lyndon Johnson, was still president of the United States. In exchange for the usual perks—government contracts and tax breaks—they gave him untraceable millions, which LBJ invested in the campaigns of sympathetic senators and congressmen from around the country, through bagmen like Bobby Baker. Heidi's little black book is full of them.

At the time, Owen was a member in good standing of what the newspapers called the "Rover Boys"—a hard-partying crowd that hung out with Clint Murchison Jr., heir to an oil fortune and principle owner of the Dallas Cowboys. Clint himself was famous for his endless womanizing,[26] and there was always a bevy of beautiful young things—whom Murchison somewhat uncharitably referred to as "half whores"—to choose from. Members of his crew served as talent scouts.

Considering Owen's own well-earned reputation as a hard-charger, it's not surprising that the affair with Heidi was soon a thing of the past. As Owen explains, it was a case of so many women and so little time.

"Course, at that time I had a hundred of them," he says. "I couldn't, you know, date one of them. But I really liked her. She was just dynamite."

"And then," says Owen, "I introduced her to one of Lyndon's guys,"—the reference being to Grady Clark,[27] a wealthy seed and fertilizer magnate from Corpus Christi—who would become Heidi's next sugar daddy.

As for Owen, he's on to another busty blonde. And, boy, is she a cutie.

Mo was a cutie, all right.

George Owen, Superstud

Her name is Maureen Kane—Mo, for short—and she was a twenty-one-year-old stewardess from California. She was lonely at the time, she says, working a late-night run from Dallas to Phoenix. "I never dated pilots—or anyone else for that matter." Then one day some friends invited her over for dinner and there was George Owen, whom she describes in her book[28] as a scout for the Dallas Cowboys and a friend of Clint Murchison.

"He was great fun," she says, "and he got along famously. And then we got very serious—*very* serious." So she quit her job, which she hated anyway, and moved in with him. A few months later, in the spring of 1967, they got married.

One story is that Mo told George she was pregnant—and George, being the gentleman that he was, offered to do the right thing. That's what Diane Wisdom says George told her. Mo, understandably, denies any such thing.

It's not that Mo hadn't had her brushes with romance before. Growing up in Mar Vista, a lower-middle class neighborhood of Los Angeles, the daughter of a former showgirl and a struggling diamond setter, she'd always longed for something better. Shortly after graduating from high school, she'd fallen for a man named G. Stedman Huard. And although at forty-one he was perhaps a bit old for her, he was a doctor to the stars, and as Mo puts it in her autobiography, "apparently quite wealthy."

For a while, they were even engaged to be married. One weekend, she and Huard flew to New York—where, Mo assures us, she did not go to bed with him. On this occasion, however, Huard gave her a 9 1/2 carat diamond ring worth $18,000, or about $135,000 at today's prices, as a token of his love.

Sad to say, the relationship soon ended. And when Mo refused to give back the ring, claiming it was a present for her nineteenth birthday, Huard sued. Mo prevailed in court and was allowed to keep the ring, which, as she notes in her book, she'd already sold anyway. However, for the cute little girl from the Notre

Dame Girls Academy in Beverly Hills, it was surely a bitter lesson of one sort or another.

Yet here she was, just two years later, preparing to give love another chance—this time with super-stud George Owen. The only problem being, she writes, that she soon realized that George was still legally married to the singer Diane Wisdom.

So she did the logical thing and returned to Los Angeles, where she married an old high school sweetheart, a stockbroker by the name of Michael Biner— meaning, of course, that she was now married to two men, Biner and Owen. However, when Biner, for reasons never made clear, couldn't bring himself to tell his family about the marriage, Mo left him in Los Angeles and returned to Owen, who by now was working in the front office and as a scout for the New Orleans Saints.

And who should she run into in New Orleans but her new friend[29] Heidi. Heidi had apparently followed Owen there too, and was busy getting to know the football team. Besides the usual stars, such as Paul Hornung, who had just been dealt from Green Bay, Heidi's little black book even includes the phone number for the Saints' practice field.

A few months later, after things fall apart with George again, Mo and Heidi travel together to Lake Tahoe to hang out for a couple of months. After a while Heidi returns to D.C., and Mo, who by this time has gotten an annulment of her marriage to Owen, heads back to L.A. to give it another shot with Michael Biner, to whom, of course, she is still legally married.

When, once again, things don't work out with Biner, Mo travels east and rejoins Heidi at Heidi's new condo—courtesy of Heidi's new Texas sugar daddy, Grady Clark—in the upscale D.C. suburb of Bethesda, Maryland.

In the summer of 1969, the two of them, Heidi and Mo, drive back across the country in Heidi's new Corvette. En route, they receive word that Biner has been killed in a car accident back in California—and although Mo doesn't say so in her book, she must have been devastated.

But at least her marital situation is now clearer. Just months before she'd been married to two men. Suddenly, at the ripe old age of 23, she is now a widow.

Back in Los Angeles, Mo promptly joins forces with another new friend, Pat Hornung,[30] a beautiful, long-legged soap opera actress she'd met in New Orleans. Mo and Pat, who was by then separated from football great Paul Hornung, get an apartment in Beverly Hills and set out to paint the town.

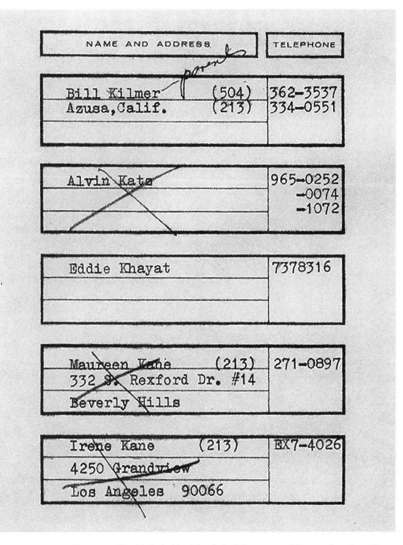

NAME AND ADDRESS	TELEPHONE
Bill Kilmer *parents* (504) Azusa, Calif. (213)	362-3537 334-0551
~~Alvin Kato~~	965-0252 -0074 -1072
Eddie Khayat	7378316
~~Maureen Kane~~ (213) 332 S. Rexford Dr. #14 ~~Beverly Hills~~	271-0897
~~Irene Kane~~ (213) 4250 ~~Grandview~~ ~~Los Angeles~~ 90066	EX7-4026

Entries in Heidi's little black book for Maureen and her mother, Irene Kane.

51

Mo and Pat Do L.A.

One of the best sources on this period is a celebrity dentist by the name of Jack Garfield.

Garfield,[31] who now lives in Palm Springs, California, met Mo in late 1969, when she showed up in his office as a patient. They quickly discovered they had a lot in common. Both had grown up in L.A. Garfield, in fact, had gone out with one of Mo's high school friends, and as Mo reminded him, had taken her friend's virginity. Soon they were dating.

Garfield remembers Mo fondly. "She was very sweet and seductive," he says, "and she had enormous breasts."[32] As he recalls, she was also quite "demure," at least by comparison with her roommate, Pat Hornung, who at the time was dating former child singing star ("I Saw Mama Kissing Santa Claus") Jimmy Boyd. One night, after a movie, he and Mo came back to her apartment to find Pat and Jimmy going at it, much too loudly, on the couch. Back in the bedroom, he says, Mo apologized profusely for her friend's outrageous behavior.

As Garfield recalls, Mo was also a good deal more genteel than Heidi, who used to visit from time to time. Mo called Heidi "my wild friend" and once described her to him as a "courtesan." One night, he says, when Heidi was in town, a group of them went to dinner at a Japanese restaurant. Heidi got drunk and started running topless down Sunset Boulevard before she could be corralled by Garfield and her date.

"Mo would never do something like that," says Garfield—but somehow, he came to feel, Mo admired and envied the older woman. "When Heidi talked dirty, I would look at Mo's eyes and I could see her thinking: 'I wish I could do that.' She wasn't disapproving, but she knew she couldn't be that way."

It was as if Mo, a good eight years younger than Heidi, had become Heidi's protégé. From the beginning, it seemed, Mo had seen Heidi as her ticket to the glamorous life that had so far eluded her. But as in all such relationships, there was a give and take.

As Garfield came to see it, Heidi was also using Mo. "Let me be blunt," he says. "When you're getting older, like Heidi was, you can use someone like Mo out front to get attention, to bring people to you. You know, someone younger, prettier, not so bright."

In fact, Heidi *was* getting older, at least by the usual party girl standards. Now approaching her mid-thirties, she was still a knockout, but she'd long since lost the dewy freshness of her nude modeling days. To acquaintances like Garfield, it was as if a tougher, business-like side has taken over. Among themselves, and to Heidi's face as well, they referred to her as the Countess.

"Mo was a pretty classy gal," says Garfield, "and we had a lot of fun together." And although they would remain friends, they soon ceased to be lovers. As Garfield explains it, "She was looking for bigger potatoes. Millionaires. I had a house in Bel Air, a Porsche. But she was looking for something more."

Mo talks a little bit about this in her book. For several months, she was hot and heavy with Jacques Bergerac, the handsome actor and heir to a French perfume fortune. In the book, there's a photo of the two of them in Las Vegas, as well as another of her with the actor Hugh O'Brian, whom she also dated.

She describes O'Brian as a "likeable, gentle, decent person," who didn't really have much of an interest in women beyond having a pretty one draped on his arm in public. There might be more to it, however. According to Garfield, Mo was distraught, when, after dating O'Brian for several months, he wouldn't marry her.

Garfield recalls the day he took out one of Mo's wisdom teeth. As he wheeled her out to the car after the operation, she was still groggy but able to talk. "You know, Jack," he remembers her saying, "I'm sick of Hollywood. Everybody here is so phony. I'm going to Washington. See if I can get a congressman or a senator or something. I've been trying for the longest time. I want to get married."

Then one night not much later, the phone rang in Mo's Beverly Hills apartment, and it was the answer to her dreams.

Nixon and Agnew at the 1968 Republican convention.

Agnew's Got a Secret

It's late November 1970. LBJ is gone, and at the helm of the ship of state—along, of course, with his trusty vice president, Spiro Agnew—is Richard M. Nixon. Tricky Dick, as his enemies like to call him.

Both, of course, will end badly. Even today, some forty years later, Nixon is among the most reviled of American presidents—as perhaps he deserves to be, although not for the reasons usually assumed. There is, for example, absolutely no evidence that he knew anything about the Watergate break-in before it occurred.

Nixonphobes should take heart, however, at the mounting evidence of his corruption. His mob ties[33] go back at least to 1950, when Los Angeles mobster Mickey Cohen raised $75,000 (about three-quarters of a million in today's money) for Nixon's first Senate race. His best friend, Bebe Rebozo, who, it should be noted, has his own bedroom[34] in the White House, also has serious mob connections.

Even at this point, less than two years into his first term, Nixon's Justice Department is negotiating terms for the release from prison of mobster and former Teamster boss Jimmy Hoffa. The estimated payoff,[35] including campaign donations as well as an under-the-table contribution to Nixon himself, will be somewhere north of $1.5 million.

It seems a little unfair, though, that Agnew has been lost in the shuffle. Forced out of office at the height of the Watergate scandal, he too was quite corrupt.[36] Since the election, he has been accepting cash-filled envelopes—in the White House basement, no less—as installments on bribes owed him from his previous job as governor of Maryland. In Maryland, for decades, it has been business as usual for companies to kick back five percent on all state contracts.

There is also the matter, unreported until now, of a call girl by the name of Pat Adams, who disappeared from the capital's party scene in 1969, shortly after Nixon and Agnew took office. At the time, her regulars included an impressive cross section of Washington political figures—senators, congressmen, generals, plus an occasional governor or two.

Carl Shoffler, in undercover guise, posing in a photo booth with his wife, Helen.

It wouldn't take long for a brilliant young D.C. police intelligence and vice officer, Carl Shoffler, to become convinced that she'd been murdered. In the underworld, at least, it was common knowledge that Pat Adams had been working for a mob-run blackmail operation, which for some time had been filming Pat and her clients.

For Pat, it was just another job—until a relatively uninteresting governor of Maryland suddenly became Vice President of the United States, at which point she apparently got stars in her eyes and tried blackmailing Agnew[37] herself.

The story goes that when word got back to Joe Nesline—who as D.C. mob boss had overall responsibility for the operation—he called in Pat's boyfriend, who happened to be a flunky in his organization. "Your bitch is talking too much," Nesline said. "Get rid of her."

Shoffler never proved his case, and we may never get to the bottom of it, either. The Pat Adams case[38] is instructive, however, because it serves to remind us that in Washington, as elsewhere in municipalities around the country, gathering sexual dirt for political leverage or blackmail is a longstanding tradition. At the city level, there's usually an understanding between the police intelligence squad and one or more of the local call girl rings. In exchange for protection from the vice squad, they're expected to provide information to the cops.

The same pattern holds in Washington, except that there are so many more intelligence agencies working behind the scenes and the stakes are so much higher. The FBI's avid interest, especially under J. Edgar Hoover,[39] in the sexual habits of American politicians is only the best-known example.

At the time, the CIA's super-secret Office of Security had its own sex squad,[40] which collected information, sometimes from the files of local vice squads and sometimes through their own clandestine operations, on the sexual habits of persons of interest. As would later be revealed, the Office of Security operated several prostitute-run safe houses around the country, fitted with two-way mirrors. Some of the safe houses[41] were used to conduct drug experiments for the CIA's "mind control" program. More typically, however, they were simply used to entertain foreign and local dignitaries, and, of course, to collect evidence for sexual blackmail. A retired New York City intelligence cop, James Rothstein— who occasionally collaborated with Shoffler on cases of mutual interest—says he was aware of three such "human compromise" operations run by federal intelligence agencies in New York City during the early 70s.[42]

The D.C. police department's sex squad was headed by long-time deputy captain Roy Blick.[43] Blick, who worked closely with both the FBI and the CIA's Office of Security, was obsessed with sex. As it happens, Carl Shoffler, the young D.C. intelligence officer who'd been nosing around the Pat Adams case, was a protégé of Roy Blick. Around the office, they even called him "Little Blick."

Blick himself was a legend among his peers. In addition to massive files on every sort of sexual activity in the nation's capital, he maintained a "sex museum" in his office. "There were all kinds of things, and he loved to show it off," recalled a former Herndon, Virginia police chief. "Pornographic pictures of every sort, and he even had an automatic fucking machine! Damndest thing I ever saw."

Welcome, then, to the Capital of the Free World—although perhaps not the same world we usually read about in our history books.

Dean Knows the Score

In her book, Mo remembers John Dean's deep, reassuring voice over the phone. He was in Los Angeles on business, he told her. An aide to his prep school roommate, Congressman Barry Goldwater Jr.—who, as Mo notes in her book, she'd also dated once upon a time—had given him her name. Would she do him the honor of having dinner with him that night?

As Mo makes clear, it was love at first sight. And although she didn't sleep with the counsel to the president of the United States that night, she says, he called her a couple of weeks later, after he returned to Washington, and asked if she'd like to spend Thanksgiving holiday with him in the Virgin Islands.

After another visit[44] by Dean, this time over New Year's, Mo flew back to Washington to be closer to the new man in her life. "I moved in with Heidi," she writes— explaining that she kept her clothes at Heidi's place and used it as a mailing address—"but I stayed with John."

In Washington, she quickly found employment as an "organizer" for a newly formed White House organization called the National Commission on Marihuana and Drug Abuse. And while this may seem a bit of a stretch, considering Mo's rather slender work record to this point, it's only fair to point out that Dean is hardly the first or last Washington official to place his girlfriend on the federal payroll.

It's a glamorous life: parties at Heidi's condo in Bethesda. More parties at Dean's and Mo's place in a newly gentrified section of Alexandria, just across the river from D.C. More often than not, Dean's Staunton Military Academy roommate, Congressman Barry Goldwater Jr., is there with his new wife Susan. Although Mo will later deny it, police intelligence learns that they've been seen at Billy's, the mob hangout.

John Dean, counsel to the president.

It's Shoffler again—the intelligence cop who's been poking around on the Pat Adams case. Mae Sullivan, the co-owner of Billy's, asks him to help her son out of a jam. He's been arrested for bookmaking. After Shoffler gets him off, Mae is his informant[45] for life. Amiable fellow that he is, Shoffler soon has Billy Rice himself giving him tips, as well.

Mae Sullivan and Billy Rice tell him that Mo and Heidi, and sometimes Dean, have been stopping by. They also talk about Heidi's work for Nesline. How he uses her to get close to NFL stars and how she worked as Nesline's "bookkeeper" in Antigua.

No question, Heidi is the mob's girl. Before the year is out, the mob will even be using Heidi to lobby[46] Dean over Hoffa's release from prison.

In February, there's a bash at the White House, headlining opera singer Beverly Sills. The dashing couple arrives in Dean's purple Porsche. Mo is wearing Heidi's full-length sable coat. Afterward, Mo calls her mom, the ex-showgirl, back in LA. "I always knew my daughter would make it to the White House!" she exclaims.

It has, indeed, been a remarkable journey for the little girl from Mar Vista—and for that matter, for Dean himself.

Just thirty-two years old, Dean has already demonstrated a truly impressive ability to navigate the treacherous political waters of the nation's capital. He's quick on his feet, a natural born political in-fighter—but most of all, resilient. He has, in fact, survived several setbacks that would have floored a lesser man.

Fired from his first job after law school for "unethical conduct"—apparently he was discovered helping a competitor file for a television license that his own firm was working on for someone else—Dean accepted a position as minority counsel for the House Judiciary Committee. Considering his career path[47] to date, just how he got the job remains a bit of a mystery. However, it probably didn't hurt that his wife at the time, Karla Hennings, whom he'd met in college and from whom he was now separated, was the daughter of a U.S. Senator from Missouri.

At the Judiciary Committee, according to a former colleague, Dean would "come in early in the morning before anybody else and go around and look on their desks to see what they were working on." And while it would be unusual for anyone in Washington not to pick up a few detractors[48] along the way, Dean seemed to have had more than his share. As another colleague from that time noted, "We all formed a rather arm's-length attitude toward John Dean because you couldn't believe him."

Entries in Heidi's little black book for John Dean and Maureen.

Then shortly after Nixon took office, Dean landed in the Justice Department with the title of Associate Deputy Attorney General. And in July 1970, following a reshuffle of jobs at the White House, Dean would become counsel to the president.

Despite the lofty title, it wasn't much more than an administrative position. Dean was charged, in addition to the duty of signing off on presidential pardons, with odds-and-ends legal tasks such as preparing citizenship papers for White House kitchen employees. In fact, although Dean's office was in the White House, it would be almost three years before Dean would actually meet with the president himself.

If Dean has learned one thing by this time, though, a job is what you make it—and he has big plans for this one. As he would write in his Watergate book, *Blind Ambition*, he knew that intelligence was the key to power in Washington, and he began positioning himself as the go-to guy in the White House.

Fortunately for Dean, he already has the makings of a small intelligence operation at hand: John Caulfield, a former New York cop hired to do campaign security work, and Caulfield's freelance employee, Tony Ulasewicz—both of whom had been providing investigative services to his predecessor, John Erlichman.

As Dean himself would later write it didn't take long for his superiors to notice that the counsel's office could perform intelligence assignments for the White House, "and we handled them while the ordinary legal work hummed along."

He gets a toe in the door[49] in April when his office is tasked with coordinating information gathering on the massive anti-war May Day demonstrations then being planned for the nation's capital. But of course he wants more.

About this time, Caulfield and Dean come up with a proposal for something they call Operation Sandwedge.[50] What they want to do is create a private intelligence firm, headed by Caulfield, that will provide the Republicans with "offensive intelligence and defensive security"—including the capability of infiltrating and burglarizing their opponents' headquarters—in the upcoming presidential campaign. They estimate that start-up costs will be $500,000.

On August 16, Dean writes a memo entitled "Dealing with our Political Enemies," in which he suggests that the White House staff start making a list of opponents for various federal agencies such as the IRS to harass. Or as he puts it: "how we can use the federal machinery to screw our political opponents."[51]

Dean is on a roll.

Phillip Bailley in law school.

Phil Bailley, Esq.

In the spring of 1971, Phillip Mackin Bailley has a one-man law office on the first floor of an old three-story brick building at 503 3ʳᵈ Street, N.W., just across from the D.C. Court of General Sessions.

Every morning he goes to court and they give him a new case. Usually it's a prostitution case, because the other lawyers don't want them. More often than not, it's another streetwalker[52] who works for the Thacker brothers, two black pimps whose headquarters are at 14ᵗʰ and U Street over a storefront church.

But that's okay with Bailley, because to tell the truth, he's a little obsessed with sex. More than a little, actually. The oldest son of a civilian air force mechanic and destined for the priesthood, Bailley had attended a five-year seminary before discovering girls and enrolling at Catholic University, in Washington, D.C., where he majored in history and lettered on the swim team. From there it was on to Catholic University Law School, where he would win the moot court and be voted the 1968 graduate "Most Likely to be Disbarred." He's five-foot six, with curly hair and a quick smile, a scamp if you ever saw one.

It's not long before Bailley meets "Jay the Lawyer," Irving J. Levine, who takes young Bailley under his wing. Levine knows his way around the courthouse. Nice suit, nice tie. Doesn't carry anything with him except an expensive leather appointment book with pink slips sticking out of it: name of the client, the charge, next court date, and that's all he needs. Levine introduces Bailley to the right vice cops. The ones who'll forget to show up for court if you slip them $50.

Bailley starts paying off the cops. Right there in the main corridor of the courthouse, while everyone is milling about: two twenties and a ten, placed in the cop's open notebook. The cop closes the notebook and sticks it in a coat pocket. That's all there is to it.

He doesn't pay them off in every case, of course, just for the Thacker brothers' top girls. He does the best he can for the rest of them—bargaining down charges, delaying the legal process whenever possible. As Bailley soon discovers, getting a "continuance" in a case is often to his benefit as well. Court-appointed lawyers get paid for each court appearance.

Levine, it seems, is something of a hound dog. He always knows the newest houses of prostitution—the high-class ones, not the ones Bailley represents—and recommends them to him. Sometimes Bailley goes, sometimes he doesn't. He's got a full social schedule of his own, after all. This is the '60s. Sex, drugs, and rock 'n' roll.

Jay the Lawyer is particularly high on this particular house, though: French and German girls who'll do anything you want, he says. A week later, when Bailley says he hasn't gone yet, Jay the Lawyer almost insists. To get him off his back, Bailley says he'll go.

It's a large townhouse in the Adams Morgan district. Bailley rings the doorbell and a middle-aged woman answers the door. Bailley tells her his name and says Jay the Lawyer sent him. That's the password.

He's ushered into a room with a big bed. Everything is a rich red or blue. There's a Persian carpet on the floor, Tiffany-style lamps and flowers in vases around the room. A woman enters the room and puts a record on the stereo.

Bailley is there, he estimates, 30–45 minutes. The next day when he sees Jay the Lawyer at the courthouse, he tells him he wants to go back again. Jay the Lawyer gives Bailley the phone number so he can make the appointment himself, and a week later, that's what he does.

This time there are three women and two other guys in the room. A stunningly beautiful blonde woman comes up to him, smiling.

"Don't be afraid," she says, with a slight German accent. "My name is Erika. Take off your clothes. We're going to have some fun."

It is, as Bailley would describe it years later, a "daisy chain gangbang." Erika, who seems to be in charge, gives the signal when it's time to change partners. She's cool and sexy at the same time.

As Bailley's putting his clothes back on, he hands Erika his card in case she ever finds herself in need of a good lawyer. He doesn't think it's very likely that she'll ever call him, because, as he knows by now, high-class operations like this one are usually well-protected. It's only the streetwalkers who ever get busted. He figures it can't hurt to try, though.

Outside, as Bailley is getting into his red Camaro convertible, parked on a side street behind the brownstone, he sees a telephone company truck and a repairman on a pole behind the house. When he looks closer, he recognizes the guy on the pole. He's a member of the vice squad, and they're obviously in the process of installing a tap on the phone. That means they're getting ready to bust the place.

Another undercover cop who recognizes Bailley from the courthouse comes over and asks Bailley what he's doing there. Bailley says it's none of his business. He's single and can do what he likes.

The cop, who apparently feels like needling Bailley a bit more, asks Bailley if he noticed that there weren't any windows in the room he was in.

"And you know why?" says the cop. "Because they were filming everything you did. How's that grab you?"

Bailley drives straight to his office. Taking a chance that the police haven't finished tapping the phone, he calls the number again and asks to speak to Erika. "Hello, Phillip," she says, "what can I do for you?" He tells her to look out, they're getting ready to raid the house.

A week later, Erika calls to thank him for the tip. There was a raid, all right. A couple of girls were taken in and booked, but she wasn't there at the time. Bailley takes the opportunity to impress her with his qualifications as an expert on prostitution law and drops a few subtle hints about how useful his cozy relationship with the vice squad might be. As he is acutely aware, representing a high-class call girl operation would be a huge step up for him.

Unfortunately, Bailley tells her, he's about to take off on a trip to California. Erika says not to worry. She gives him her phone number and tells him to give her a call when he gets back.

Call Me Kathie

Bailley can't believe his luck. Here he is, twenty-nine years old, a fledgling lawyer at the bottom of the D.C. legal food chain—and this beautiful blonde creature with a body right out of *Playboy* apparently desires his legal services. Or maybe even his company.

It's another case of a nice Catholic altar boy going off the rails. If not all sex is bad, the reasoning seems to be, then the opposite must be true. On one hand, it's kind of endearing, if only because Bailley's so eager. On the other, it's anything but—because Bailley, who has pursued this line of reasoning to its logical conclusion, has come up with the not entirely original idea that his way to fame and fortune in Washington is to become a pimp on the side. His idol is Lyndon Johnson's bagman, Bobby Baker, whose Quorum Club until recently had been a source of female companionship for Washington's elite. In fact, in his own penny-ante way, Bailley has already embarked upon such a career. He and several of his drinking buddies have formed a group called Subway Properties, the ostensible purpose of which is to gather inside information on the D.C. subway system, which was then in the early planning stages, and to buy up properties where the stations were going to be built.

In practice, however, their meetings are little more than an excuse to get drunk and have sex with women Bailley has obtained for the occasion through ads in local college newspapers. When one of them, a Maryland graduate student named Astrid Leeflang, becomes a regular at the Subway Properties get-to-gethers, Bailley asks her if she'd like to be a glamorous call girl one day. To Bailley's surprise, she's all for it.

Bailley, now in his early 70s and living in Florida, acknowledges the error of his ways. "I was corrupt," he says sadly but matter-of-factly. What he doesn't need to say is that he was so inept at it.

So of course, when he returns from California, Bailley calls Erika right away. Erika says she'll be delighted to come see him. All she requires is that he fix her something to eat and have some good champagne on ice.

By now Bailley has an apartment on the third floor of a new apartment complex in southwest Washington. He's chosen the place because it's a hot spot for singles action. After all those years in the seminary, Bailley has a lot of making up to do.

When Erika arrives, Bailley guides her to his balcony and uncorks a bottle of Moët & Chandon, which he has determined is classy enough for the occasion. While he grills the steaks, they engage in small talk about his trip to California.

Smooth operator that he is, Bailley soon steers the conversation to business. In case she missed it before, he tells Erika how he routinely bribes some of the vice squad not to show up in court.

Erika asks Bailley if he thinks he can get them to tell him what they're working on as well. He says he doesn't see why not.

Below them is a large swimming pool surrounded by government girls in bikinis, soaking up the late afternoon sun. To the east, they can see the roof of the Supreme Court building and the Library of Congress.

"Phillip," she says, "I can trust you. I want to level with you. My real name is Kathie Dieter."

Bailley thanks her for trusting him and tells her she won't be sorry. Then they adjourn to the bedroom.

Before she leaves, Kathie Dieter tells him she has some exciting plans on the drawing board. As soon as everything is solid, she says, she'll let him know.

Of course, as is now perfectly clear, Bailley is being played for a fool. For starters, his new client is lying to him about her name. There is no Kathie Dieter. It's a cover.

Erika, the name she gave him when he first encountered her at the townhouse, would be a little closer to the truth. At least that's a street name—the name she used as stripper and, at this time, is still using on her business card: Erika L. Rikan, Business Services Consultant. Except, of course, she isn't now, and never has been, a business consultant in any ordinary sense of the term.

Both Heidi's close friend Josephine Alvarez, and Heidi's sister, Kathie Dickerson, remember quite clearly that at this time—in 1971 and 1972—Heidi sometimes used the name Kathie Dieter.[53] By then, Josephine had left Nesline and moved back to Miami, but she'd stay at Heidi's condo in Bethesda whenever she came to town. She remembers hearing Heidi use the name when she accompanied her to a hairdresser's appointment.

Kathie, who would have been fifteen at the time, also remembers hearing Heidi use the name, probably to make an appointment over the phone. Although she knew that Heidi used different names from time to time, it struck her as odd this time because, of course, Kathie was really her name.

Heidi, her sugar daddy Grady Clark, and Kathie, dining in Las Vegas.

Setting Up the DNC

A week or so later, Kathie Dieter—or Heidi, as we should now call her to keep things straight—calls Bailley's office and leaves a message with the secretary for Bailley to meet her that evening at Nathan's, the hot new singles bar in Georgetown.

As it happens, Bailley's secretary is his seventeen-year-old sister, Jeannine. In the early '70s, it would have been considered déclassé for a lawyer, even a sole practitioner like Bailley, not to have a secretary. So Bailley enlists his younger sister. She's young and inexperienced, but Bailley is lucky to have her working for him. She's as sensible and responsible as he is not. Her recollections[54] about the phone calls—like those of Josephine and Kathie about Heidi's used of the alias "Kathie Dieter"—will later be important evidence in this case.

At Nathan's, Heidi tells him about her new operation. It's up and running now, she says, and it's at the Columbia Plaza, a luxury apartment complex near the State Department and the Watergate. She's already getting business from State. She says she'll put him on the payroll—$200 every two weeks—to report to her on the activities of the D.C. vice squad.

Eager to please as always, Bailley chimes in that they might be able to hustle up some business at the Watergate, too. As he happens to know, that's where the offices of the Democratic National Committee are located. In 1968, he'd been a volunteer on Bobby Kennedy's campaign, working as a scheduler in the speaker's bureau. Just the week before he'd stopped by the DNC to offer his services again for the upcoming presidential campaign. The presidential campaign is gearing up, he tells her, and it won't be long before the DNC offices will be teeming with party functionaries, away from home and looking for a good time.

Heidi picks up on the idea immediately. To make it happen, though, she says, they'll need someone on the inside to direct the fun-seeking Democrats to her operation at the Columbia Plaza. Bailley says he'll get right on it.

So Bailley starts hanging out in the Watergate bar, where he knows the DNC secretaries go after work. He'll sit down next to a couple of them at the bar and strike up a conversation. After a while he says, "Say, bet you've got a lot of horny guys coming through here." When they say "You aren't kidding" or something like that, he takes it a step further: "Wouldn't it be neat if you could find a way to help them out?"

After about a week of getting nowhere, the girl Bailley's talking to gives him something besides a blank stare. So he presses forward and tells her he's looking for someone to make a few phone calls. He notices she's drinking champagne—just like Kathie. He takes it as a good sign.

"It's nothing illegal," he says, "just an escort service. Just girls wanting dates. I'm sure you'll be paid $50 every time you call." All she's got to do is show them a plastic folder with photos of some of the girls, then direct the visitor to a phone in an office, which, as Bailley has already determined, is usually empty.

Next time at Nathan's, Bailley tells Heidi about the break-through and gives her the girl's phone number. Heidi makes arrangements for someone to meet the girl at the Watergate bar and give her the photos.

They give the girl a code name and Bailley writes it in his own address book: Champagne.

Heidi invites Bailley to drop by the Columbia Plaza operation, which turns out to be a one-bedroom apartment on the third floor. The décor—Tiffany lamps, red and blue furnishings—is remarkably similar to what he saw at the brownstone townhouse on 17th, where he first met Erika. He assumes it's part of the same operation.

He takes out a joint and lights it. "Do you need that stuff?" she says, "It's illegal for crissake. People can smell it."

Bailley pushes her back against the bed and starts to fondle her. She slips away. Obviously, it's all business now, although Bailley is given to understand that the other girls will be available to him from time to time. She wants to discuss the DNC operation. She says that with all the new business they expect to get, they'll be expanding soon. This will just be their headquarters.

Bailley gives her a rundown on what the vice squad is doing and she pays him $200.

Washington, D.C., looking down on the Watergate, and behind it, the Columbia Plaza.

Drinks at Nathan's

Heidi calls Bailley's office and leaves another message with Jeannine, telling Bailley when to show up at Nathan's.

This time when Bailley walks into Nathan's there's another woman sitting at the bar with her: blondish, shoulder-length hair, heavy make-up, long red fingernails. He recognizes her from a photo Heidi had shown him at one of their earlier meetings, which showed Heidi, a woman named Crissie, and the younger, blond woman now before him, all doing a chorus line pose on a beach at Lake Tahoe.

Now here she is. In the flesh, to use words that spring instantly to Bailley's mind. To Bailley, who admittedly has an over-heated view of the world, her pants look like they're sewn on. You can see the outline of her ample breasts. To Bailley, she looks like a woman who wants to be picked up. But then, so does just about every other woman in the place. It's a singles bar, after all, and this is the '70s.

Heidi introduces the woman in the sewed-on pants as Mo Biner. She says she's going with someone in the White House who's got a lot of clout. As Bailley recalls, Mo doesn't have much to say. Heidi does all the talking. After the meeting Bailley puts her in his address book under the codename "Clout." Next to that he writes the initials, "M.B."

Mo, it should be made clear, denies any part of this. In a 1996 deposition,[55] taken in connection with one of the lawsuits in this case, she says she never met Phillip Bailley. Not at Nathan's or anywhere else. In the same deposition, it's also worth noting, she also attempts to portray Heidi as a casual friend she rarely spent time with. Obviously, one of them—Bailley or Mo Dean—is not telling the truth here, so it's up to the reader to figure out which one that is.

In addition to Bailley's bi-weekly report on the vice squad, there's also a running discussion of how to recruit new girls for the operation.

Of course, the professionals are already on board. What Heidi wants, though, is to recruit a crew of amateurs—"first-timers," she calls them. The professionals—"experienced bitches"—are too jaded. The "first-timers," she says, are still excited by the action and eager to please.

Seizing the opportunity, Bailley suggests that she give Astrid Leflang, the University of Maryland student, an audition. After hearing Bailley's stories about Astrid's promiscuous adventures at the Subway Properties parties, Heidi turns her down as too low-class. Bailley, however, is not discouraged. Washington is full of young women, looking to fall in love with suitably powerful men.

As Bailley recalls, Heidi spends a lot of time at the Watergate bar, making new connections. All she has to do is convince them that it's okay to broaden their horizons and live a little.

As each new girl is recruited, Bailley adds her to his book. Beside each code name, he writes down their initials, in case he forgets who the code name belongs to.

Lou Russell, private eye.

Man in the Closet

In late September 1971, Heidi leaves a message for Bailley to meet her at two p.m. at their new quarters on the sixth floor of the Columbia Plaza. When he knocks, the door is opened by a big guy in his fifties who introduces himself as Lou. Lou tells Bailley that Kathie has been delayed but will be there as soon as she can, so Bailley should just kick back and enjoy himself. There's booze on the breakfast bar and deli sandwiches in the refrigerator.

While Bailley pours himself a JB and water, he looks around. It's a three-bedroom apartment with a window looking out at the Watergate, a block away. Sofas, oriental rugs, Tiffany-style lamps. Coffee tables with magazines arranged on them.

Lou tries to strike up a conversation about sports betting. Bailley, who's not really much of a gambler himself, says he bets on Notre Dame and the Redskins. "That means you bet with your heart," says Lou. "That's not smart."

Soft rock music is playing on a radio. There's a sports show on the television. Lou answers the phone and starts talking with someone about placing a bet on the Redskins game.

In the living room, there's another guy, about Lou's age or maybe a little younger, sitting on a sofa, eating a sandwich. He's wearing a turtleneck sweater and looks like he stays in shape. After he finishes his sandwich, he stands up and walks toward the bedroom at the end of the hall. Beyond him, through the open door, Bailley catches a glimpse of a brass bed with a canopy cover. The man walks through the door and Bailley loses sight of him. The door's still open, but Bailley doesn't see him moving around in the room.

Bailley doesn't know what to make of it, so after another JB and water and a toke or two, he determines that he should find out what's going on. After all, he is Kathie's lawyer, and it's his job to advise her on how to keep things as legal as possible. So he walks down the hallway and pokes his head in the room. The guy in the turtleneck is nowhere to be seen.

Bailley opens the bathroom door. Nothing there.

Then, on a whim, Bailley opens the closet—and there he is, sitting in a chair, surrounded by recording equipment. There's a reel-to-reel movie camera pointed at bedroom, which you can see on the other side of what Bailley figures must be a fake mirror.

The man jumps up, instantly angry. "What are you doing here? Get out," he shouts. "You're drunk." He pushes Bailley back out of the tiny room. "If you know what's good for you, you'll forget you ever saw anything."

Embarrassed and mystified, Bailley goes back to his seat at the breakfast bar. Lou is grinning. "I see you've discovered another part of the set-up," he says. "Now you do have to wait till Kathie gets here."

About a half hour later when Heidi finally arrives, Lou briefs her at the door. She comes over and sits behind Bailley. "Well, Phillip," she says with a knowing smile, "I see you've made yourself at home. How do you like the set-up so far?"

Bailley, who by now has had a couple more JBs, explodes. Some forty years later, this is how he remembers the conversation. Of course it can't be word-for-word, but for him it's as real as if it had been recorded on the spot:

"Kathie, what the hell's going on? There's a guy in the closet. God knows what he's up to."

Kathie—Heidi, of course—stays cool.

"Let's start over," she says. "This is Russ," gesturing toward the man who introduced himself to Bailley as Lou. "He does a little of everything. Generally he keeps the lid on things. But it's my operation, and you're my lawyer, so calm down and listen."

Yes, she says, they're filming the johns. As she reminds Bailley, this should hardly come as a surprise to him. He already knew about the townhouse on 17th—so what's the big deal? "It's so we can keep the politicians and high-rollers in check," she says. The people behind it—the "cowboys," as she calls them—are working to save the country.

"So stop worrying," she says, "we're protected by the big guys." Then she needles him a bit. "Phillip, I thought you were ready for the big time. This is the big time. Are you my lawyer or not?"

Bailley fixes himself another drink. Pretty soon a young woman arrives and exchanges a few words with Kathie. She's dressed to kill—cleavage down to here. Bailley figures her for a dancer. Not much later there's a knock on the door. Lou—or Russ, as Bailley has now learned to call him—answers the door and a well-dressed man in his forties enters the apartment. Smiling coyly, the girl takes the man back to the bedroom at the end of the hall.

By now, even Bailley knows he's in way over his head.

For starters, there's Lou Russell, the guy who greeted Bailley at the door. A down-and-out private eye with the rheumy eyes of a heavy drinker, he lives in a Q Street apartment with the telephone down the hall.

Bounced years ago from the FBI because of his alcoholism, he got a job rooting out commies for the House Un-American Activities Committee. That ended in 1954 when he got caught trying to shake down[56] a witness, the actor Edward G. Robinson, for a "loan." For the past decade-and-a-half or so, he's been making a living doing whatever comes his way. Some jobs are just a little dirtier than others.

One of Russell's current clients is the Washington attorney Bernard "Bud" Fensterwald. Every so often, Russell drops by Fensterwald's office[57] and regales the staff with funny stories about taping a bunch of hookers at the Columbia Plaza. The prostitutes, he says, are cooperating in the venture. They're getting clients from the DNC, he tells them. You wouldn't believe some of the stuff he's hearing.

What should have Bailley scared, though, is that Russell is currently working for a company called McCord Associates, owned by Russell's old friend James McCord.

A former high-ranking officer in the CIA's Office of Security, McCord, at least according to the official records, has been retired from the CIA for about a year now. And you can believe that if you want to. But whether the retirement is fake or not, the fact is that old spooks like McCord always retain their Agency contacts, so it really comes down to the same thing. In fact, McCord still has a case officer[58] and is reporting regularly to his bosses at the Agency.

What Bailley has stumbled into appears to be nothing less than a CIA sexual blackmail operation. Certainly, it has all the earmarks. We may never know for sure, if only because at the height of the Watergate scandal—despite a specific request from a Senate committee attempting to pursue the CIA's role in Watergate—the CIA simply destroyed[59] all its records of its internal taping system.

Kathie and Heidi, circa 1972.

We've Got Two Kathies

More meetings: "Champagne," the DNC secretary Bailley enlisted to handle the phone calls to the Columbia Plaza, is leaving. A replacement must be found. The girl who takes over her duties is named Ida Wells. Bailley gives her the code name "Iron Works" and writes it down in his address book.

Also, they now have a connection with a well-placed White House secretary who has access to the "Green Book"—the schedule of society balls and other exclusive social events attended by the movers and shakers in the new administration. They call her the "Greenhouse Nymph."

Heidi's plan to include amateurs—"first-timers," as she calls them—is also moving along. At one of the meetings—Bailley can't remember whether it's at Nathan's or the Palm, another Washington hotspot where they've started to gather—there's a new girl. "Candy Cane," as Bailley puts her down in his book, works with Mo on the federal anti-drug task force. Bailley, hard-charger that he is, has always understood that Mo is off limits, because she's with a mysterious figure called "Clout," but he determines to give Candy a shot.

A week later, there's a message for another meeting, this one at Nathan's, too. When Bailley arrives, Heidi and Crissie,[60] the other girl in the Lake Tahoe photo, are sitting at a table in the restaurant area behind the bar. With them is a young teenage girl wearing a little too much make-up for her age.

"Well, now," says Bailley, being his usual charming self, "who is this beautiful young lady?"

The girl looks up from her drink, obviously pleased to be noticed. "Kathie?" she says.

Chrissie chimes in: "Yes, Kathie. We have two Kathies here now."

"Yes, precious," the woman Bailley knows as Kathie Dieter says to the girl. "This is our lawyer, Phillip Bailley. Now he's got two Kathies to deal with. Me, and now you."

The other Kathie, of course, is Heidi's younger sister, Kathie Meck, who would have been visiting Heidi then. Every vacation, Heidi would fly her to wherever she was at the time. Kathie, who had just turned fifteen, doesn't recall the details of the conversation, but does remember meeting a short man named Bailley at the restaurant. At the time, Kathie still thought of her older sister as a "model," because that's what she'd always been told.

After a few minutes, the young Kathie and Crissie go off to the restroom together and Bailley lays into Heidi. He's already on edge over the filming at the Columbia Plaza. Now it looks like she's brought an underage girl into the operation. If there's anything that might attract the attention of an otherwise lackadaisical vice squad, that would be it.

"What are you doing?" he demands. "It's dangerous. She's jailbait."

Heidi calms him down. Yes, she says, she's under-age, but there's nothing to worry about because the girl isn't involved in the Columbia Plaza operation. "And she's not going to be," she says. "She's a very special friend."

"Phillip," she says with a smile, "you worry too much."

Jeb Magruder, acting chairman of the Committee to Re-elect.

Magruder's a Wuss

Sandwedge goes down in flames. Dean's superiors won't go for it because they don't think Caulfield's the right man for the job. But not to worry. Dean's still on track to become the go-to guy at the White House on intelligence matters.

In October, Dean dispatches Caulfield to New York to get Xaviera Hollander's little black book.[61] Hollander, who would later promote herself with a book called *The Happy Hooker*, is running a high-class prostitution operation, catering to the rich and famous. Caulfield gets the book, all right, but her clientele includes as many prominent Republicans as Democrats, so it's of no political use.

It's not a total bust, though. Dean lets his colleagues in the White House know he's got the goods. In his own Watergate memoir, he writes about needling press secretary Ron Ziegler, whose name, he coyly suggests, is in the Happy Hooker's little black book.

And there's still Ulasewicz, the other member of Dean's intelligence team.[62] Dean doesn't usually deal directly with the crusty former NYC detective, and it's probably just as well. As Ulasewicz would later write in his own book *The President's Private Eye*: "Every crease in his suit was perfectly ironed, every hair on his head in place, and he had a smooth, almost hairless face. Everything about him appeared too delicate and too neat for me. I took an instant dislike to him and dismissed him as a slick operator."

The same month, Caulfield assigns Ulasewicz to look into a new movie called *Richard*. The movie, billed as a "satirical spoof" on the president, stars a comedian who does a very funny impersonation of the president and has, in fact, legally changed his name to Richard M. Dixon. Ulasewicz is supposed to see if opposition political groups are behind the movie.

When none are found, Dean writes a rather lame memo noting that Dixon's agent "asserts the film will not be insulting" to the President. And while that's not much, at least it's a reminder to the higher-ups that he's plugging away—and isn't that what it's all about?

And if Dean can't persuade his superiors to give him the go-ahead on Sandwedge, there's more than one way to skin a cat.

Over at the newly formed Committee to Re-elect the President, acting chairman Jeb Magruder[63] is looking for a general counsel, and he makes the mistake of asking Dean for help finding one. Magruder, an eager-to-please public relations type, is no problem for a guy like Dean.

Sure, says Dean. But why not combine the functions of legal counsel and intelligence? Magruder, bless his heart, is all for it.

In November, Dean sets up a meeting with Gordon Liddy,[64] a highly eccentric former FBI agent and New York State prosecutor, who, it seems, is enamored of everything about the Third Reich. Liddy is currently employed at the White House as a member of its Special Investigative Unit, the "Plumbers"—so called because it was set up to combat recent leaks of classified information to the press.

As a matter of fact, Liddy and Howard Hunt, another supposedly retired CIA agent now working for the White House, have recently burglarized a psychiatrist's office in California, looking for files on one of the psychiatrist's clients, Daniel Ellsberg. It was Ellsberg, of course, who leaked the Pentagon Papers to the *New York Times*.

As is apparent from Liddy's own account of the meeting, he doesn't much care for Dean, either. What bothers him, apparently, is Dean's longish hair, "hanging shaggily down over the collar of his suitcoat." As a dyed-in-the-wool conservative at this moment in American history, Liddy would not have been able to abide any male with long hair. Liddy also doesn't like what he describes as Dean's "ferret-like face." There is obviously something about the ambitious White House aide that turns a lot of people off.

Dean doesn't waste time with small talk. There's an election coming up next year, he says, and they've got to be ready with a "first-class intelligence operation."

"You mean Sandwedge?" says Liddy. Over the past few months, he's had several discussions with Caulfield, and knows all about the plan, including its provisions for electronic surveillance, black-bag jobs and other covert operations.

"No," says Dean, "we're going to need something much better, much more complete and sophisticated than that."

"You're talking about a hell of a lot of money," says Liddy.

"How's half a million for openers?" says Dean.

Liddy tells Dean he's certainly in the ballpark, anyway: half a million for openers, and probably another half before they're finished.

"That doesn't bother you?"

"No problem," says Dean.

Candy's New Boyfriend

It's a fall afternoon in 1971, and Bailley is on his way to an appointment with "Candy Cane." She's the executive office employee, a friend of Mo, who's been recruited as a part-timer for the operation—a real '60s girl, into yoga and massage. In fact, just the sort of "first-timer" Kathie Dieter has been looking for. She has a massage table, which she brings to the Columbia Plaza occasionally, and her specialty is blowjobs.

Like Bailley, she lives in a large apartment building in Southwest D.C.— just around the corner from Bailley, as a matter of fact, so Bailley can walk.

Bailley is still some distance away when he sees her on the sidewalk in front of her building, talking to a dark-haired man in an overcoat. The man is standing next to an official-looking black sedan with a driver in the front seat. As Bailley watches, the man in the overcoat gets into the back seat of sedan and drives off. Bailley catches up with "Candy Cane" as she's going back inside her apartment building.

"Hey, Candy," he says, "congratulations. Now your boyfriends have chauffeurs. Who was that big shot?"

"You weren't supposed to see that," she says. "That's the boss of bosses."

At the time, Bailley doesn't know who she's talking about. Some time later, he will recognize the dark-haired man from a photo in the *Post* as Jeb Magruder, head of the Committee to Re-elect the President—or CREEP, as liberals like Bailley like to call it.

"You should forget what you saw," says "Candy Cane" as she and Bailley ride the elevator up to her floor. Inside the apartment, the massage table is already set up.

Here, once again, we have a difference of opinion on some basic facts. "Candy Cane," who is now a respectable lawyer in another city, denies that any such event ever occurred. She also denies ever having known Bailley. She admits

DATE	NAME AND ADDRESS	TELEPHONE

McDONALD, HERB
CAMEO CIRCLE
LAS VEGAS, NEV.
GREG McDONALD

AREA CODE 702
NUMBER 878-7773
AREA CODE 213
NUMBER 397-8772

LINDA MEYER
BROTHER 751 0600
AREA CODE 362 0313

JEB MAGRUDER
4814 FT. SUMNER DR.
NUMBER 202
AREA CODE 229 3065

#104 PATTY MASON
4948 SENTINEL DR.
SUMNER, MD 20016
NUMBER 229 6248
AREA CODE

WORK 625 7291

STUART MILLER
AREA CODE
NUMBER
338 672

Entry in Heidi's little black book for Jeb Magruder.

having lunch "once or twice" with Heidi and Mo, but insists that she had no idea at the time that Heidi was in the call girl business—which is a bit odd on the face of it, since Mo, who was their only friend in common, knew very well what Heidi did for a living.

It is also significant that "Candy Cane," as we will call her here because there's no need to embarrass her for what seems to have been a youthful indiscretion, also appears in Heidi's little black book. She is, in fact, listed twice—and at the address where Bailley says he saw her talking with Magruder that day.

Magruder, now a broken man[65] in his late 70s, and living with his daughter in Connecticut, has resisted several attempts to get his side of the story. Most recently, he failed to respond to a certified letter asking him how his name, address, and unlisted phone number ended up in Heidi's little black book.

Considering the role that Magruder would play in the Watergate break-in as chairman of the Committee to Re-elect, his presence in Heidi's book is hardly insignificant. However, as is also worth noting, he is by no means the only Nixon administration official whose name shows up there.

In addition to Magruder and Dean, there's Secretary of Commerce Maurice Stans. Also Fred LaRue, a close friend and aide of Attorney General John Mitchell, with an address and phone number in the Watergate apartments.

And of course, Dean's prep school roommate Congressman Barry Goldwater Jr. and their circle of friends, including Dean's White House colleague Fred Fielding, and their down-the-street neighbor, Senator Lowell Weicker.

The more straight-laced Magruder could hardly be part of that social set, but it's certainly possible he might have met Heidi or one of her girls at the parties they were privy to now that they had access to the Greenhouse Nymph's social schedule. Or perhaps the arrangements were made through the White House protocol office,[66] which, according to a former White House aide, was "always using those call girls at the place next to the DNC."

Although Heidi's list of Republicans was nowhere near as extensive as the line-up of Texas Democrats she cultivated during the LBJ years, she was clearly making inroads into the new administration.

Nacht und Nebel

Gemstone is a doozy, all right:

A team of prostitutes operating from a boat anchored offshore from the Democratic convention in Miami. Electronic surveillance of rival candidates, and break-ins and burglaries at their campaign headquarters—although, it should be noted, there's no mention of the Democratic National Committee offices. Liddy doesn't think there's anything there worth the trouble. Liddy has named each section of the plan for a precious or semi-precious stone: Ruby, Crystal, Quartz, Sapphire.

And, oh yes, Diamond: a plan to kidnap demonstrators outside the Republican convention. Then drug them and hold them in Mexico until the convention is over.

Dean and Magruder are sitting in John Mitchell's office at the Justice Department, as Liddy presents the plan[67] to the Attorney General. Mitchell is being briefed because only someone of his rank can approve a budget as large as $1 million. For each new gemstone program, there's a professionally done chart,[68] which Liddy places on an easel before them.

On the Diamond chart is the German phrase *Nacht und Nebel,* "night and fog," which as Liddy knows was a Nazi program for kidnapping resistance fighters in occupied territories. As the chart indicates, kidnappings will be carried out by a "Special Action Group."

"What's that?" says Mitchell.

"*Einsatzgruppe, General,*" says Liddy, using the hard *g* as a proper German would. Liddy is assuming that Mitchell, who would have been familiar with World War II history, will know that the *Einsatzgruppen* were SS death squads.

Gordon Liddy, intelligence team leader.

Mitchell spends some time fiddling with his pipe before speaking. "Gordon," he says, "a million dollars is a hell of a lot of money, much more than we had in mind. I'd like you to go back and come up with something more realistic."

Of course Liddy is upset. Dean had promised him a million bucks—"no problem" —when he signed on. But he really doesn't have much choice.

Dean isn't about to give up, either. He tells Caulfield he wants someone to case the DNC.[69] Dean will later deny doing any such thing. Caulfield, however, certainly has no doubts about whether it happened or not. And neither does Ulasewicz, who writes that he got a call from Caulfield, telling him to come back to Washington.

"For what?" says Ulasewicz.

"Dean wants you to check out the offices of the Democratic National Committee."

"For what?"

"He just wants to know how it's set up."

So Ulasewicz flies down to Washington. He walks into the DNC, says hello to the receptionist, and tells her he's waiting for someone to join him. That way he doesn't have to tell her who he's there to see. Then he takes a seat where he can see everything that's going on.

As it quickly becomes apparent, the office is just a glorified political record-keeping and mail-order operation. So he makes his excuses and leaves, then he calls Caulfield.

"There's nothing there Jack," he says. "They're not worried about security. It's as open as the sky."

Why, you have to ask yourself, would Dean's memory fail him on something like that?

James McCord, Watergate burglar and saboteur.

Howard Hunt, CIA agent.

Who Are Those Cowboys?

Heidi's assurances notwithstanding, Bailley is still quite worried. Who are these "cowboys," anyway? He knows he's into something dangerous, but what's he supposed to do? If he got out now and turned them all in, the very least that would happen to him is that he'd lose his bar license and probably go to jail.

Not that Bailley's seriously thinking about getting out, anyway. For the ex-seminarian, the vibe of illicit sex, glamour, and power is simply more than he can resist. So he does the logical thing and tries to take the edge off with more ganja and Scotch. When Bailley wakes up in the morning, his bed is soaked with sweat.

Sometimes when he drops by the Columbia Plaza, he hears Russ and one or another of the cowboy types joking about the "passionate squeals" on the tapes they've been making. "Better than a professional porno flick," says Russ.

Bailley knows where they keep the key to the closet. It's in one of the kitchen cupboards, because he hears a rattling there whenever one of the cowboys says it's time to get back to work. He also knows that except for a maid named Margie, there's not supposed to be anyone there in the morning—but he's got to be sure.

So one morning in February, about 11 o'clock, he knocks on the door. When Margie answers, he introduces himself as Kathie Dieter's lawyer and says he's going to meet her later. Can he hang out in the kitchen? Margie—who, as it turns out, also has a slight German accent—says sure, make yourself at home. Kathie Dieter has already told her about him.

Bailley spreads out some papers on the kitchen table and pretends to study something while Margie goes about her work. After a while, she leaves with an armload of laundry, saying she'll be right back. Bailley gets up to check the cupboard. The key is there, all right, hanging on a cup hook. He's tempted to try the closet door, but it's a good thing he doesn't because Margie comes back sooner than he expected. Next time he'll know.

Next time, he goes to the closet as soon as Margie leaves. Cassette tapes are everywhere: Some neatly stacked in boxes, some strewn on a shelf built to hold the camera and recording equipment. Each tape has a white label with the number of the tape and a time and date written on it in black ink. On the desk, there's a log listing the tape number and the name of the john and one or two words describing the nature of the sex act.

Bailley snatches a tape from the shelf and slips it into his breast pocket. Then he hurries back to the kitchen, puts the key back on the hook, and he's sitting at the table when Margie returns.

Of course, Bailley tells himself he's doing this because he has a duty, as Kathie Dieter's lawyer, to fully understand the extent of his client's legal liability. And, who knows, he may even believe himself at the time. But the real reason is that he's dying to hear the tapes.

Back in his apartment, Bailley pours himself another drink and shoves the tape into a recorder he's purchased just for the purpose. He recognizes the girl's voice immediately. It's Linda, one of the pros.

She starts by asking for the john's ID. "Just to make sure you're not a cop," she says. Then she reads from the ID into the hidden microphones: name, address, height and weight. Maybe a comment or two about the size of his cock, just to get things rolling.

Then comes the sex talk and the passionate squeals Russ and the cowboys have been laughing about. For Bailley, it's like a live porno show. He plays the tape over and over, getting more worked up each time.

Next time Bailley meets up with Kathie Dieter, he watches her carefully for signs she knows about the missing tape. When he doesn't detect anything, a few days later he makes another foray into the closet. Before long, he's got a collection of about twenty tapes.

At first he tells himself he's just borrowing the tapes. As Kathie Dieter's lawyer, he needs to know what's going on. Now that it's time to return them, though, it occurs to him that maybe he shouldn't. If the Columbia Plaza operation ever gets busted, they'll be his insurance policy—something he can use to bargain his way out of trouble.

Bailley remembers something the Thacker brothers told him: if you ever want to hide anything from the law, wrap it in aluminum foil and put it in the freezer, marked "steak." He wraps some of the tapes in foil and puts them in his refrigerator.

The rest of them, he puts in a second briefcase, along with a file he's started keeping on the Columbia Plaza operation. Wherever he goes, he carries two briefcases— one for his current cases, one to get out of jail free.

Dean Pipes Up

Dean and Magruder are back in Mitchell's office, listening to Liddy take another go at Gemstone. With Hunt's help, Liddy has cut the Gemstone budget to $500,000.

They've eliminated a couple of big-ticket items, such as a plane to follow the Democratic nominee's airliner and intercept messages. However, the prostitutes, kidnappings, electronic surveillance, and burglaries at the campaign headquarters of the two leading Democratic candidates—Muskie and McGovern— as well as McCloskey, a renegade Republican, are still on the table. This time, Mitchell says he'll have to think about it.

At which point, Dean pipes up.[70] "Sir, I don't think a decision on a matter of this kind should come from the Attorney General's office. I think he should get it from somewhere else —completely unofficial channels." At least, that's how Liddy remembers it.

Dean himself has a slightly different version. As he recalls in his book, he clears his throat and says, "I don't think this conversation should go on in the Attorney General's office."

Either way, it's the old deniability game. The advantages for Mitchell are obvious. If things ever hit the fan, he can always claim he never signed off on anything.

But it's an even bigger boon for an ambitious underling like Dean. Because if the Attorney General is no longer in the loop, then who's left to make these completely unofficial decisions? Of course Dean will still have to go through Magruder, but he won't be much of a problem.

Dean may already have Magruder by the balls, anyway. It's entirely speculative, of course, but considering Dean's close friendship with Heidi, it's hardly possible that he doesn't know that one of Heidi's girls is having an affair with Magruder. Dean may have even set him up in the first place. And if that's so, he also knows that the last thing the straight-laced Magruder would ever want is for his shameful secret to be exposed.

It's been three months now since Dean first told Liddy to set up Gemstone—and still no action. For a guy like Liddy, this has got to be aggravating. Plus, he's got to deal with Hunt, the supposedly retired CIA guy who's been so helpful to him. Hunt's on his case because he's got a team of ex-CIA soldier-of-fortune types in Miami lined up for their little project, and he can't keep them dangling forever.

It is, by the way, basically the same crew that conducted the burglary of Ellsburg's psychiatrist's office[71] in California the previous year, with Liddy and Hunt standing guard outside. Although they would tell Liddy they didn't find anything, that was a lie. As Liddy would later realize, whatever was taken in the burglary went straight to Hunt's contacts in the CIA.

All of Hunt's Miami team have CIA backgrounds. One of them, Eugenio Martinez, is actually still employed by the CIA, and is reporting to his case officer on his adventures with the White House intelligence team.

On his own, Liddy will also add an electronics surveillance expert to the crew. It's none other than James McCord, the recently retired CIA agent. Since he's already been doing some security work for the White House, McCord is an easy hire. As careful readers will remember, McCord is also the employer of Lou Russell, the down-and-out private investigator who's supervising operations at the Columbia Plaza.

There is, in fact, credible evidence that McCord and Hunt actually know each other from the Bay of Pigs days. For Liddy's benefit, however, they pretend they've never met before. The CIA, it seems safe to say, has effectively taken control[72] of Liddy's little intelligence unit—and Liddy doesn't have a clue.

In February, Magruder informs Liddy his budget for Gemstone is now $250,000. To meet the new bargain basement constraints, Liddy and Hunt toss out everything except a couple of spies in the enemy campaigns, two prostitutes to work the democratic convention in Miami, and the burglaries of the campaign offices of McCloskey, McGovern, and Muskie. Then Liddy presents it to Magruder.

According to Liddy, Magruder has just one change to suggest. He asks Liddy if it might not be possible to bring the prostitutes up to Washington and put them to work right away. Liddy tells Magruder that bringing whores to Washington would be like shipping cars to Detroit.

But Magruder doesn't seem to want to let the subject go. If he can find a reason to go to Miami, he says, could Liddy fix him[73] up with one of the girls down there?

"Jesus," says Liddy to himself, "the wimp can't even get laid with a hooker by himself." Then he thinks again and tells Magruder that since he'll be paying for it anyway, if Gemstone is approved, he can take his pick.

From the look on Magruder's face, Liddy gets the idea that if Magruder has anything to say about it, Gemstone will be approved.[74]

Astrid Spills the Beans

If Heidi has told Bailley once, she's told him a million times: stop worrying so much. We've got friends in high places. We're protected. Nothing's going to happen.

But Heidi's wrong—although in fairness to her, it's nothing she could have foreseen. Already, an investigation is underway.

Remember Astrid Leeflang, the University of Maryland grad student who told Bailley she wanted to be a glamorous call girl? For a while there, Bailley even tried to get her a job at the Columbia Plaza, but Heidi turned her down because she wasn't classy enough.

Not wanting to hurt Astrid's feelings, of course, Bailley doesn't tell her she was no longer in line for the glamorous call girl job. He just passes her on to other members of the infamous Subway Properties group. Understandably, Astrid is starting to feel misused and betrayed.

Several months later, she's telling her sad tale to a couple of D.C. vice detectives. When she gets to the part about Bailley's mysterious high-class call girl operation, that really gets their attention.

On the morning of April 6, 1972, Bailley is in court, preparing to make an opening statement in yet another misdemeanor case when the phone rings on the clerk's desk. The clerk hands the phone to the judge, who listens for about half a minute before handing the phone back. "Mr. Bailley," he says, "this better not be one of your acts to get a continuation."

Bailley takes the phone from the clerk. It's Jeannine on the other end, informing him that the FBI is at this very moment raiding their law office. From what she's been able to make out from their conversations back and forth, the FBI is at his apartment as well.

They took the phone books, she says. As luck would have it, just that morning she'd begun the process of transferring the names in Bailley's book to the one she kept in the office. So she had both of them on her desk when agents arrived. They'd scooped them up right away, along with the office phone log. What she wants to know is how can she run an office without the phone books?

Bailley tells her to stay calm and he'll get back to her. He's not as upset as he might be because he's already had a couple of tokes this morning.

At his apartment, Bailley assesses the damage. They've taken a hookah, a stack of *Playboys*, and his collection of naked photographs. Amazingly enough, though, they've missed the tapes he'd been taking from the closet at the Columbia Plaza. They're still in the back of his freezer, wrapped in aluminum foil, marked "Steak."

From the pay phone in the basement laundry room, Bailley calls Heidi. He tells her the FBI got his phone books, but they didn't get his Columbia Plaza file. He had his briefcase with him in court. Heidi tells him to take everything to the beach and burn it, then meet tomorrow afternoon at Nathan's.

That night, Bailley drives to Ocean City on the Eastern Shore of Maryland, past Bobby Baker's Carousel, past all the places on the beach where he and his Subway Properties buddies used to party. When he's sure he's not being followed, he parks and walks out onto the sand dunes. He starts a fire with his cigarette lighter and feeds the contents of the Columbia Plaza file into it. But when it comes time to burn the tapes, he finds he can't part with them. He puts them back in his briefcase and drives home to D.C.

They called her the Countess.

Connecting the Dots

The next afternoon at Nathan's, Heidi is already waiting in a booth when Bailley arrives. She's wearing a tight blue sweater, black fitted pants, lots of perfume, and she does not look happy. She starts in on Bailley as soon as he sits down.

Surely, she says, he realizes by now that he's been taken down by his own personal lifestyle. Fucking anything that walks. Smoking marijuana in front of anyone and everyone. What did he expect?

"Did you burn the whole damn file you were keeping?" she demands. Bailley says yes. He doesn't consider it a lie, because the tapes weren't part of the file. When he brings up the phone books again, she says she's not worried. "We can handle all that," she says. "It's no problem."

She tells Bailley he will be getting no legal help from her people. "This has nothing to do with us," she says. "Take care of yourself," she says. "I hope your lawyer can put out the fire for your sake, Phillip, I really do."

It's beginning to dawn on Bailley that he's being fired. She's cutting him loose.

They're there for almost an hour, with Kathie—Heidi—doing most of the talking, drinking one glass of champagne after another. Occasionally, to make a point, she smacks her hand on the table.

She asks the waitress for the check, then leans closer so Bailley doesn't miss a word. "Remember one thing," she says. "We've got nothing to do with your legal problems and you're not going to drag us into this. We won't allow it. Understand? I know you do. You're a smart guy."

For the first time, Bailley realizes he's afraid of her.

It doesn't take long for investigators to connect the dots. The phone numbers in Bailley's books and the office phone log lead to names and addresses.

According to Jack Rudy,[75] the Assistant U.S. Attorney assigned to prosecute the case, the FBI would soon determine that "employees at the DNC . . . were assisting in getting the Democrats connected with prostitutes at the Columbia Plaza."

At various times, Rudy has been remarkably forthcoming on the topic. More than a hundred people were subpoenaed to the grand jury. As he would tell author Jim Hougan, "We had them coming up and down the back elevator to my office so no one would see them. They were beautiful girls,[76] and they were terrified of being connected to Bailley's activities."

Some of them, as Rudy makes clear, were part of Bailley's social network and some were tied in with the Columbia Plaza operation.

"One of the girls we interviewed talked about high level government officials who were using the facilities," Rudy would say in a 1986 interview, adding that he was in a "negotiating position[77] with [a woman he spoke of as] Kathie Dieter and another girl" at the time.

In an interview with author Len Colodny in 1989, Rudy would recall some of the code names in Bailley's phone books. The "Greenhouse Nymph" was one, he said. Another was "Clout." Around the office, Rudy said, they referred to the "Clout" entry as "Mike Bravo"—which, as he explained it, is military lingo for the initials "M.B.," which were written next to it.

In the tape-recorded interview, Colodny asks him if he can remember what M.B. stood for.

"We knew that to be a lady by the name of—oh, hell—that was Biner, Binner, Bomer, no . . ."

"Biner?" says Colodny.

"Biner," says Rudy.

"Maureen Biner?"

"Yeah," says Rudy. "I've identified it. That's Maureen Biner."

As Rudy would go on to tell Hougan, another interviewee was Lou Russell,[78] the down-and-out private investigator who'd been managing daily operations at the Columbia Plaza. Russell, he said, went out of his way to interest him in another house of prostitution several blocks away on DuPont Circle.

Although it became obvious to Rudy that Russell was just trying to divert his attention from the Columbia Plaza, he opened a file on the DuPont Circle operation as well. A subsequent investigation determined surreptitious filming was going on there. In fact, several local judges were being blackmailed.

Not too surprisingly, however, no charges were ever brought against the DuPont Circle blackmail operation.

Or for that matter, the one at Columbia Plaza.

As Rudy's superiors at the Justice Department soon let him understand, the DNC phase of the investigation is a "political time bomb."[79] It's time to move on to "more important things."

Burglary #1

About the end of April, Liddy gets a message to report to Magruder at his office. Liddy arrives in a grumpy mood, expecting more non-Gemstone related assignments that will further draw down on the approved budget. He is, however, not prepared for this:

"Gordon," says Magruder, "do you think you could get into the Watergate?"

In their discussions so far, no one has mentioned Watergate, but Liddy knows what he means. As he writes in his book, he's been thinking about burglarizing the DNC, too—but later, after the Democrats finish their convention in July. That's when the winner would start using it as a campaign headquarters.

Sure, says Liddy. It can be done, but isn't it a little early?[80]

Magruder doesn't miss a beat. "How about putting a bug in O'Brien's office?" he says. Larry O'Brien, of course, is the DNC chairman.

"For that, it's a bit late," says Liddy. As Liddy and Magruder both know, O'Brien had already moved his base of operations to Miami. In fact, Liddy and Hunt's team has been trying to figure out how to bug him down there.

"Okay, so he's in and out," says Magruder. "There's still plenty of activity over there. We want to know whatever's said in his office, just as if it was here, what goes on in this office."

Liddy thinks it's all a bit strange but he agrees to do the job.

"The phones, too," says Magruder. "And while you're in there, photograph whatever you can find."

Liddy wants to argue, but it's clear to him that Magruder is just relaying orders.

"Get in there as soon as you can, Gordon. It's important."

On May 22, a Monday, Hunt's crew arrives from Miami. They check into a run-down hotel on 14th Street and spend the next few days checking out the city. They stop by the Watergate office building, take the elevator up to the 6th floor, and, from the hallway, take a look at the DNC offices. They also stop by the Howard Johnson Motor Inn, directly across the street from the Watergate. That's where the bugs will be monitored, once they've been placed inside the DNC.

On Friday, using aliases, they check into the plush Watergate Hotel, which adjoins the Watergate office building. That night they throw a catered party for themselves in one of the hotel's banquet rooms. The idea is to stay there until all the waiters have gone home, then make their way through a basement corridor to the Watergate office building—but somehow, there's a screw-up.

As Hunt and McCord explain to Liddy the next day, they had to wait so long for the lights to go out in the DNC, an alarm was activated along the corridor route, making it impossible for them to carry out the mission. A decade later, researchers would realize that no such alarm[81] ever existed.

Saturday night, they try again. The burglars actually enter the Watergate office building. Back at the HoJo command post, everything is looking rosy—at least until Liddy is informed that they weren't able to get into the DNC offices because their lock-picking expert, Vergilio Gonzalez, didn't have the right tools.

With the benefit of several decades of hindsight, and of course all the research that's been done in the interim by Hougan, Colodny, and James Rosen, the author of a more recent revisionist work, *The Strong Man*, it's clear that the CIA boys are doing everything they can to sabotage the White House mission. At the time, though, Liddy doesn't catch on. He orders Gonzalez to fly back to Miami to get the proper tools. Gonzalez returns Sunday afternoon. That night they try again—and the third time's the charm.

Or at least, that's how it seems. Two bugs have been installed in the DNC. One on O'Brien's phone, the other, as it turns out, on the phone of an obscure DNC functionary by the name of R. Spencer Oliver—whose phone, as Liddy could not have known at the time, is the one being used to set up dates for visiting politicos at the Columbia Plaza.

The following Wednesday, when Liddy hasn't heard anything from Mc-Cord on the bugging operation, he makes a visit to the HoJo listening post to see what the problem[82] is. McCord informs him that one of the bugs, the one on O'Brien's phone, doesn't seem to be working, possibly because a steel girder is blocking the signal.

They have, however, located the second signal, and it's now coming in loud and clear. McCord points to a man in the shadows who, he says, is monitoring the transmissions. The man is wearing headphones, and as McCord explains it, taking notes on what he hears. Then he passes the notes on to McCord, who edits them.

Understandably perplexed, Liddy asks McCord why he doesn't have the receiver hooked up to a tape recorder. When McCord, the longtime CIA surveillance expert, gives him a cock-and-bull story about how his tape recorder is incompatible with the receiver, Liddy asks him why he doesn't go out and buy another tape recorder. McCord tells him not to worry. Once Liddy has had a chance to look at the logs, he'll see that the system is working just fine.

The logs are useless. Nothing but snatches of phone conversations of "DNC secretaries," gabbing about their social lives. Even Magruder can see it's a waste of time.

On June 9, a Friday, he tells Liddy they've got to go back in to replace the defective bug.

Evening Star

WITH SUNDAY MORNING EDITION

NIGHT FINAL

WASHINGTON, D. C., FRIDAY, JUNE 9, 1972   Phone 484-5000   CLASSIFIED 484-6000   CIRCULATION 484-5000   10 Cents

ll-Girl Ring Uncovered

ley "compelled, induced and endured" the girls to observe in prostitution.

J least eight women were abused in the ring, according to sources.

ant. U.S. Atty. abn Rudy chief of the office's grand section, said the names of women were not disclosed the indictment because of brutalies such disclosure it cause their employers their families.

he said, however, they all be called to testify at trial.

spokesman for the U.S. orney's Office said the case been under investigation

by the FBI and the grand jury section for about three months. It was brought to the attention of law enforcement officials, the spokesman said, when a woman who had been enlisted for the ring complained.

According to sources, the operation involved only "available girls"—most of them had just broken up with their husbands or boyfriends.

The sources said Bailey allegedly recruited the women by first dating them, then offering them marijuana and wine, supposedly a powerful combination of stimulants. He

See INDICTMENT, Page A-4

clines

Govern

By PAUL HOPE
Star Staff Writer

Sen. Edmund S. Muskie said today that Sen. George S. McGovern probably will win the Democratic presidential nomination, but that he would not endorse him at this time.

Muskie spent predictions that he would get behind McGovern and thereby virtually assure nomination of the front-running South Dakota senator.

Muskie, himself the former leader in the race for the nomination, listed two main reasons for not throwing his weight behind McGovern.

He said it would subvert the party reform processes for selecting a nominee, which are

Attorney Philip M. Bailey talks to a reporter in his District apartment today after his indictment as the alleged head of a call-girl ring here.

GLEASON IS DEFENDANT

Blue Law Suit Filed

Evening Star, June 9, 1972.

A Visit to the White House

Bailley's luck has just run out. His picture is at the top of the front page[83] of Friday's Washington *Star,* under the wildly misleading headline: "Capitol Hill Call Girl Ring Uncovered."

"The FBI," the story begins, "has uncovered a high-priced call girl ring allegedly headed by a Washington attorney and staffed by secretaries and office workers from Capitol Hill and involving at least one White House secretary, sources said today."

Bailley has been indicted—although not, as a closer inspection of the records reveals, for anything even remotely related to Heidi's Columbia Plaza operation or a "high-priced call girl ring" of any sort. The 22-count indictment against Bailley deals solely with Bailley's alleged transgressions against four of his former girlfriends. There is, however, no way of knowing[84] that from the indictment itself because none of the alleged victims are named.

According to the *Star*'s anonymous source, who at least got this right, Bailley has been accused of recruiting them to prostitution "by first dating them, then offering them marijuana and wine, supposedly a powerful combination of stimulants. He then induced them to pose for 'personal' photographs—some of them nude—which Bailley allegedly said would be for his personal use . . ."

It is, to be sure, deplorable. However, as the indictment itself indicates, Bailley can hardly be considered a big-time pimp. In fact, the only dollar amount listed in the indictment is a single payment of $25, which to this day, Bailley contends he thought someone was giving him for sodas and chips while Astrid was upstairs entertaining the troops at a Subway Properties party.

If it weren't for the fact that Bailley was now looking at charges that could land him in federal prison for several years, it would all seem a bit quaint.

But headline writers do what headline writers must—and besides, it seems that the *Star*'s unnamed source is trying, in typical Washington fashion, to get at least some of the story out there. In addition to the "White House secretary"—who, as the story notes, is not named in the indictment "because her case did not involve crossing state lines"—the story also mentions an unnamed "White House lawyer" who is somehow involved.

It is therefore hardly surprising that when, back at the White House, John Dean gets his copy of the afternoon paper, he goes on red alert. He immediately summons the prosecutors—John Rudy and Rudy's immediate superior, Don Smith—to the White House, instructing them to bring the case file with them. He even sends a limousine to pick them up.

In later years, in what appears to be an attempt to downplay the significance of the meeting, Dean will say he remembers the visit,[85] but only vaguely. He also tries to make it appear that he didn't set it up himself.

In fact, however, Dean's own phone log for that day, Friday, June 9, has Rudy's and Smith's names on it. And certainly, Rudy has no problem remembering his chauffeured visit to the White House that day, down to the grey pin-striped banker's suit and blue shirt that Dean was wearing at the time.

As Rudy would recall,[86] the first thing Dean wants to know is who leaked the story to the press. When Rudy says he doesn't have a clue, Dean says he thinks the Democrats are behind it. In fact, some forty years later, we still don't know who the source was. However, given the mixture of fact and error in the newspaper story itself, the most likely candidate would be a cop or FBI agent who didn't want to see the matter swept entirely under the rug.

Dean then asks about the White House lawyer and White House secretary in the news story. Rudy doesn't know who the secretary is, but the lawyer is a woman named Connie, who works in the Office of Emergency Preparedness. Since the Office of Emergency Preparedness is part of the executive branch, she is technically attached to the White House.

In fact, Connie is another one of Bailley's girlfriends, who hasn't done anything more illegal than show up in Bailley's address book and pose for a naked photograph, which was among those seized when the FBI raided Bailley's apartment.

Next Dean turns his attention to Bailley's phone books and tells the prosecutors that he'd like to keep them over the weekend to study. When they turn him down—since it would, of course, be an obvious violation of the law for them to part with evidence in an on-going case—Dean asks a secretary to copy them. Then, for the next forty-five minutes or so he proceeds to study the books, circling names as he goes.

Considering Dean's closeness not just to Mo, but Heidi as well, it is first of all barely conceivable that he isn't already aware of Heidi's Columbia Plaza operation, or for that matter, Bailley's connection to it. But even if he isn't, we can only imagine his distress when he sees the entries for "M.B." or "Clout," along with what must be familiar phone numbers.

And that being the case, if Dean is as smart as we have every reason to believe he is, he realizes this could easily develop into a full-blown, career-ending sex scandal.

Before the end of business Friday, Dean will put a call in to Connie's boss at the Office of Emergency Preparedness, and Connie will be allowed to resign.

As Dean's phone log for June 9 shows, he also calls a fellow named Roemer McPhee, a Washington lawyer and counsel to the Republican National Committee, who happens to be the administration's back channel[87] to a newly appointed federal judge, Charles Richey. As it also happens, Richey has just been assigned to Bailley's case.

The following Monday morning, Liddy is once again sitting in Magruder's office. To Liddy's annoyance, because he figures this sort of thing should have been dealt with long ago, Magruder starts asking questions about the file cabinets in the DNC. Liddy is attempting to answer, when suddenly Magruder becomes quite animated.

"Here's what I want to know," says Magruder,, slapping the lower part of his desk with his left hand.

Liddy understands immediately what he's talking about, because that's the drawer where Magruder keeps derogatory information on the Democrats. In the past, whenever Magruder has called him in to his office to discuss a new investigation, that's where he's gone to retrieve whatever information he already has on hand.

"I want to know what O'Brien's got right here," says Magruder. "Take all the men, all the cameras you need. *That's* what I want to know."

Somehow, over the weekend, the DNC mission has changed from replacing a bug to photographing all the files in O'Brien's office.

When Liddy informs Hunt, Hunt is incredulous. "All of them?" he says. "It'll take hours."[88] Hunt calls his team in Miami and tells them to get ready.

THE WHITE HOUSE
WASHINGTON

TELEPHONE MEMORANDUM

June 9 , 19 72

TIME			NAME	ACTION
	PLACED	DISC		
OUT	AM		Ed Morgan	
INC	PM		Tom De Caira	
OUT	AM		Acree	184 X 2101
INC	PM		Joe	
OUT	AM			
INC	PM		Mike Norton	Jon Rose
OUT	AM			
INC	PM		David Aaron	
OUT	AM		Judy	
INC	PM		Roemer McPhee	
OUT	AM			
INC	PM		Bud Krogh	
OUT	AM			
INC	PM		Jim Nolan	654 - 8682
	PM		Rudy	
	PM		Earl Silbert 426-7481	426-7511
OUT	AM			
INC	PM		Jack Caulfield	
OUT	AM		Ron Ziegler	
INC	PM		Pat Gray	175 X 3444
OUT	AM		Alex Butterfield	
INC	PM		Darrell Trent	to V. d. (904) 255-6911

Dean's phone log for June 9, 1972.

U.S. District Court Judge Charles Richey.

No More Loose Ends

On Thursday morning, Bailley is in U.S. District Court, standing in front of Judge Richey. The clerk reads the charges and Bailley pleads not guilty. Bailley's lawyer, Edwin C. Brown, then asks that Bailley be released on his own recognizance.

It's the prosecutor Jack Rudy's turn to speak.[89] The government has no objection to that, he says, "subject to certain conditions"—one of which is that Bailley be committed to St. Elizabeth's Hospital, the District of Columbia's mental institution.

Rudy then asks the judge if they might adjourn to Richey's chambers, with no reporters or spectators present, so the judge can consider a motion ordering Bailley's commitment.

"Well, I think we can do that," says Richey. "I would like to hear whatever you have. If you want me to do it in camera, I would be delighted."

Another judge might not have been so accommodating. But Richey, as shall soon become apparent, is not just another judge. Appointed to the federal bench barely a year before, with no prior judicial experience at any level, he is a product of the corrupt Maryland political machine.

News stories at the time of his appointment identify Richey as a "close friend"[90] of Vice President Agnew. It was, in fact, Agnew who, as governor, appointed Richey to his previous position as general counsel for the Maryland Public Service Commission.

In a state where, as Agnew's subsequent prosecution would reveal, it was accepted practice to collect a five percent kickback from companies doing business with the government, Richey would have been the bagman for all the utilities and the bus and taxi companies under the commission's umbrella. Although Richey would never be charged with anything so rude as public corruption, it's safe to say he hadn't achieved his current position by crusading against the institutional corruption that has surrounded him his entire political career.

Behind closed doors, Rudy begins his argument. Witnesses, he says, have told him that Bailley "ranged from being weird in his actions to outright paranoia."

"Now, of course, these weren't expert witnesses," he continues. "These were male and female persons who were associated with Mr. Bailley going back to 1969. But they found in their association with him that his conduct was bizarre at times and . . . that he was very boisterous and radical in his approach to treating different subjects like politics, social mores, and so forth."

Rudy then moves on to a discussion of the evidence seized from Bailley's apartment.

"The government's proof will show that Mr. Bailley took photographs of females, a wide variety of females, in the nude. Some of the females were asked to engage in various acts such as putting whipped cream on their bodies . . . This was done at Mr. Bailley's request for the purpose of exciting Mr. Bailley at a later time when he could look at these photographs, giving him a thrill, so to speak, beyond the normal act of sexual intercourse."

To make his point, Rudy shows the photos to Richey, one after another.

"This is Mr. Bailley again, asking the same female to put whipped cream on her body. Those are Mr. Bailley's feet at the bottom . . . The female told me it was Mr. Bailley's idea then to eat the whipped cream off her body."

"Here is another whipped cream shot other than the ones I have shown you. That is a different female."

In addition, Rudy continues, in Bailley's apartment the FBI also discovered several examples of what he terms "commercial pornography," including "a number of motion picture films."

"One of the films deals with an unknown male and female who are engaged in oral sodomy and sexual intercourse in living color."

Having thus concluded his case, Rudy once again asks Richey to commit Bailley to St. Elizabeth's—*sua sponte*, which is Latin for "on his own volition"—"to see whether he is competent to stand trial, but more importantly, to see whether he suffered some mental disease or defect at the time that he is alleged to have committed these acts."

"I believe your honor will have to agree," says Rudy, "that it is a very unusual case."

Judge Richey couldn't agree more. "Obviously, it is unusual. Before going any further, let me ask this question. Is this a case that has to be tried? Is there any possibility that something can be worked out to serve the ends of justice in terms of society, as well as Mr. Bailley?"

"Not from our standpoint," says Bailley's lawyer, Edwin Brown. "There is no disposition by way of a plea to any of the counts involved."

"We do not deny that Mr. Bailley went out with various young ladies. We do not deny that he engaged in certain sexual acts with certain young ladies. These acts were done on a consensual basis."

Moreover, he says, he has no intention of arguing that Bailley is not guilty by reason of insanity. He intends to take the case to trial.

It is time now for Judge Richey to make his ruling. He notes, first of all, that he considers Mr. Brown a "very able defense counsel." Furthermore, he has "a high regard for him for his professional capacity and judgment."

"On the other hand," says Richey, "I think the court has a larger duty in this or any other case, regardless of what defense counsel or government counsel may say in any matter, and that is to see that justice is done . . .

"In view of the showing made by the government this morning, the court feels that the interests of justice do require that the accused be examined at the earliest possible date. I would be inclined to sign the order."

Before he adjourns the secret hearing, however, Richey has one last piece of business. He places a gag order on Bailley, his lawyers, and the prosecution.

So much for loose ends. Bailley, the one person who might be foolish enough to blow the whistle on the Columbia Plaza operation, has not just been discredited. He's about to be buried.

St. Elizabeth's, the mental institution for Washington, D.C.

Burglary #2

The next day, June 16, Hunt's team arrives from Miami and checks in at the Watergate hotel. Liddy has scheduled the break-in for ten p.m. When that time rolls around, however, the lights are still on in the DNC. The burglary will have to wait.

At 10:50 p.m. McCord gets things rolling.[91] Under the pretext of delivering a typewriter to the Federal Reserve, he signs in at the Watergate security desk and takes the elevator up to the eighth floor. Then he walks down the stairwell, taping the locks open as he goes—on the sixth floor, where of course the DNC is located, on B-2 and B-3 in the basement, and finally, the underground garage. The burglars will enter the stairwell from the garage.

After McCord finishes the taping, he stops by Liddy's and Hunt's command post —Liddy has also rented a room in the Watergate for the occasion—and says he'll let them know when the coast is clear. Then McCord returns to the listening post at room 723 in the HoJo.

Another hour goes by, and someone's still working in the DNC. As it turns out, it's just an intern named Bruce Givner, taking advantage of the office's pre-paid long-distance phone line to call friends back home.

Shortly before midnight, a new Watergate security guard, Frank Wills, checks in for the graveyard shift. When Wills makes his rounds, he discovers the tape on the B-2 and B-3 basement doors. He removes the tape, then calls his supervisor, who tells him to check the other floors, too. If there's tape on any other doors, there might be a burglary in progress. Otherwise, it's probably just something left earlier in the day by a maintenance worker. The supervisor tells Wills to call back and let him know.

At 12:05 Givner, having finished with his phone calls, turns out the lights in the DNC and takes the elevator to the lobby—where, who should he run into but Frank Wills, the security guard. The two of them strike up a conversation, and Wills—obviously figuring that any further door-checking can wait—goes with Givner across the street to get a cheeseburger at the HoJo.

Everybody, it seems, is going to the HoJo restaurant. About this time, Alfred Baldwin, who's been listening to the phone intercepts for McCord in Room 723, heads down for two hot fudge sundaes. When he returns at about 12:45, according to a subsequent FBI interview, McCord is on the phone with the command post, telling them the lights are still on in the DNC.

Clearly, that's a lie.[92] The lights have been off for about forty minutes now.

Finally, at about 12:50 p.m., McCord calls the command post again to say the coast is clear and that he'll be right over. It takes about five minutes to walk from the HoJo to the Watergate, so when McCord doesn't show up for fifteen minutes or so, Liddy asks him why.

McCord says it's because he stopped by the underground garage to make sure the basement door locks were still taped. Everything's fine, he says. Everyone wishes everyone else good luck and the burglary team departs on its mission.

Once again, McCord is lying. There is now no tape on the basement doors—Wills having removed it more than an hour ago—and McCord would have known this if he'd stopped by to check.

When the burglars—Barker, Sturgis, Gonzalez, Martinez, and McCord—arrive at the basement door and find the tape gone, McCord has some explaining to do. What he says is it must have been removed in the last ten minutes.

McCord, Barker, and Martinez then head back to the command center to find out what to do next, while Gonzalez stays behind to pick the lock. Sturgis stays with Gonzalez to stand watch.

Back at the command post, Liddy confers with Hunt and McCord. Hunt, unsettled to hear about the missing tape, thinks the mission should be aborted. McCord says he wants to get it over with. In his opinion, the tape was probably removed by a repairman. Liddy sides with McCord, and McCord, Barker, and Martinez head back to the garage to try again. As they do so, however, Barker and Martinez lose sight of McCord. Somehow he just disappears.

When Barker and Martinez arrive back at the basement entrance, Gonzalez and Sturgis are gone. Gonzalez has already picked the lock and the door has once again been taped open. So Barker and Martinez walk up the stairwell to the sixth floor, where Gonzalez and Sturgis are trying to open the door to the DNC. For some reason, Gonzalez is having trouble picking the lock.

When McCord arrives about five minutes later, Martinez asks him if he remembered to remove the tape from the basement door on his way up. Obviously, if the night watchman finds the doors taped again, it'll be a dead give-away.

Yes, says McCord, he removed the tape.

Gonzalez is still having trouble with the lock. Finally, he and Sturgis simply take the door off its hinges. Flashlights on, the burglars enter the DNC.

About this time, security guard Frank Wills remembers he's supposed to check the basement doors again—and of course when he does, he discovers that they've been re-taped. Once again, he calls his supervisor. At 1:47 a.m., Wills calls the police. At 1:52 a.m. the police dispatcher is on the radio, asking for a unit to respond to a possible burglary at the Watergate.

As luck would have it, there's an unmarked car just a block and a half away. Inside the car, a young undercover cop by the name of Carl Shoffler—remarkably enough, the same young cop we met earlier in the case of missing call girl Pat Adams—grabs the handset. "We got it," he says, and he and the two other undercover officers also in the car hightail it for the Watergate.

After speaking with Wills, the cops head up to the eighth floor.

Across the way, in Room 723 at the HoJo, Baldwin gets on the walkie-talkie to tell Liddy he sees flashlights on the eighth floor. Together they decide it must be the Watergate security guards, making their two a.m. rounds.

A few minutes later, Baldwin gets back on the horn. "Now they're on the seventh floor," he says. There's a pause. And then, as Liddy puts it so elegantly in his book, "a query, in a wondering tone that made its way through even the low fidelity of the transceiver."

"Say, any of our guys wearin' hippie clothes?"

"Negative," says Liddy. "All our guys are in business suits."

"They're on the sixth floor now," continues Baldwin. "One's got on a cowboy hat. One's got on a sweatshirt. It looks like . . . *guns!*"

Back at the command post, Liddy tries to raise the burglars on their walkie-talkie.

"One to two. Are you reading this? Come in."

No answer, so he says it again.

"One to two, come in. That's an order."

Back comes the whisper: "They got us."

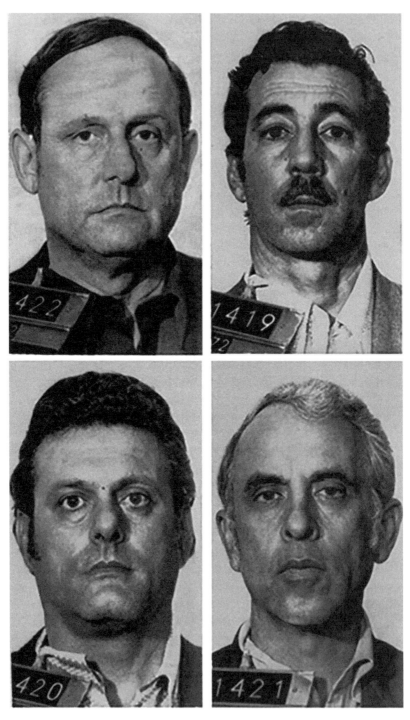

The Miami crew, clockwise from upper left:
Bernard Barker, Virgilio Gonzalez, Eugenio Martinez, and Frank Sturgis.

The Key to Watergate

And the rest, as they say, is history—although, as we should expect by now, not necessarily the cookie-cutter version that's come down to us over the past forty years. As usual, the reality is much more interesting—all the more so once we accept the fact that we really don't know what's going on here.

For example: What is McCord up to? As should already be apparent from the first unsuccessful burglary, McCord and the other CIA guys have been intent on sabotaging the White House's efforts from the beginning. But what, exactly, is McCord trying to accomplish with all this lying?

In his groundbreaking book, *Secret Agenda,* which was published in 1984, Jim Hougan makes a good case that whatever McCord is doing—lying, delaying, disappearing—has everything to do with employee Lou Russell, who, it will be remembered, has been managing things at the Columbia Plaza call girl operation.

Indeed, Russell has been lurking in the shadows[93] of Watergate the night of the break-in, driving back and forth from his daughter's house in Maryland. At one point, he even tells his daughter that he has to leave to meet with McCord.

As Russell will subsequently admit to the FBI, he even whiled away a couple of hours in the HoJo coffee shop—although he insists his only reason for doing so is that an old girlfriend of his used to have her hair done across the street at the Watergate beauty salon, and he wanted to relive those days. This is, of course, another cock-and-bull story, and the FBI investigators know it, but they can't prove it.

Hougan surmises that McCord's lies that night are meant to cover for the times he slipped away to confer with Russell—who, Hougan also suggests, is playing a part in McCord's last-ditch attempt to scuttle the break-in, even if it means getting the burglars arrested.

Of course McCord has no intention of getting arrested himself. His calculation has to be that since he only has to replace the bug, he'll be long gone when the cops arrive. However, there's a slip-up—maybe a double-cross—and McCord is trapped inside the DNC offices. And if, as it appears, there's a double-crosser, then the primary candidate for that role is obviously Russell, the down-and-out drunk, who's already proved himself more than willing to work for anyone who's got money.

The closer we look at the Watergate burglary, the cloudier everything becomes. It would be a mistake to assume that we know what the burglars were actually supposed to accomplish that night. All we can really be sure of is that it didn't have much to do with Larry O'Brien—because when Shoffler and his cohorts burst in, they aren't in O'Brien's office at all.

Instead, their cameras have already been set up in the main room, on a desk belonging to a DNC secretary named Ida "Maxie" Wells. As readers may remember, Maxie Wells is the young woman, who, according to Bailley, ended up with the job of directing prospective Columbia Plaza clients to the phone in an empty office in the DNC.[94]

All of which might be dismissed as an interesting coincidence, if it weren't for the fact that as the cops are lining up the burglars to search them, feet spread, hands against the wall, one of them does a very strange thing—and he's lucky he doesn't get himself killed over it.

From behind, Shoffler can see Eugenio Martinez slipping a hand inside his jacket. For all Shoffler knows, he's going for a gun.

Shoffler slams Martinez in the back, shouting at him not to move. When Martinez persists, Shoffler grabs him and wrestles him to the ground. Then he searches him to see what the burglar could have considered important enough to risk his life for.

In the breast pocket of Martinez's suit coat, Shoffler finds a notebook with a small key taped to the back of it. As the FBI will later determine, the key fits the lock to Maxie Wells's desk.

It is, of course, the key to Watergate—although you'd never know it from the more conventional Watergate histories. For them it doesn't even exist—because if it did, they'd have to acknowledge that there's much more going on here than fits neatly into their own theories.

And then there's Shoffler, the super-duper intelligence cop, who just happens to be waiting near the Watergate when the call goes out from the dispatcher.

He's not even supposed to be on duty that night. In fact, he's supposed to be in Pennsylvania, preparing to celebrate his birthday with his family the next day.

Instead, though, when his regular shift ends at ten p.m, he volunteers for overtime duty, and gets himself assigned to an undercover crew patrolling the Watergate area. They're sitting in a car about a block from the Watergate when they get the call for a burglary in progress.

Shoffler grabs the speaker. "We've got it," he says, and he and his two partners that night head to the scene of the crime.

What is Shoffler doing there? Or perhaps more to the point, who is he really working for?

Shoffler had signed on with the D.C. police straight out of Army intelligence. His last military assignment, before taking a job with the police, was at the National Security Agency's "listening post" outside D.C., responsible for intercepting communications from embassy row. Like so many players in the intelligence game,[95] he undoubtedly maintained a dual allegiance, even while working for the D.C. police.

For the rest of his life, Shoffler would maintain his being there was simply a coincidence. There are many, however, who believe he was tipped off that night. And that list includes not just a former snitch[96] of his who's written a book about it, but two of Shoffler's former partners[97] on the D.C. intelligence squad. One of them, Karl Milligan, is also aware that Shoffler knew Lou Russell, who, of course, is a leading candidate here for whistle-blower. James Rothstein, the former NYPD intelligence cop who sometimes worked with Shoffler, says Shoffler once told him he was tipped off about the burglary—although when pressed, Shoffler only hinted at his source.[98]

And then there is Captain Edmund Chung, Shoffler's former commander in Army intelligence, who testified before the Senate Watergate Committee that Shoffler told him the arrests resulted from a tip—and that if he ever went public with the truth, "his life wouldn't be worth a nickel."

Shoffler, of course, denied ever saying such a thing, and there the matter rested. Like most other inconvenient discrepancies in the Watergate record, Chung's testimony was dismissed as a misunderstanding.[99]

Clearly, though, it's not mere happenstance that Shoffler was parked outside the Watergate on the night of June 16.

Watergate cop Carl Shoffler, working the street.

John and Mo get married with Heidi as bridesmaid.

John and Mo Get Hitched

It's still early morning when Shoffler puts in a call to the *Washington Post*'s night police reporter. Two young Metro page reporters, Bob Woodward and Carl Bernstein, are members of the team that write the story for the next day's paper. And although they don't get a byline on it, it will be the first of many Watergate stories for them.

Over the next three years, with the assistance of their mysterious informant "Deep Throat," they will blaze a journalistic trail straight to the President himself—largely by exposing the cover-up, which, of course, the White House almost immediately puts into play.

For most fans of the movie *All the President's Men*—by far the most popular version of the saga—this is, in fact, where the Watergate story begins.[100] Except for some tying up of loose ends, it's where this story ends.

If, as Dean insists, he didn't have anything to with the break-ins, he is certainly running the cover-up from day one. On Monday, he meets with Liddy and tells him everyone will be taken care of. Over the next week, he meets three times with the CIA's deputy director Vernon Walters, trying to persuade him to get the CIA to put up the hush money. When that doesn't work, it's up to the White House fundraisers to raise the cash. Over the next three months, Tony Ulasewicz, Dean's and Caulfield's old private eye, will distribute upwards of half a million[101] dollars to the burglars' lawyers and to Hunt's wife, setting up clandestine meetings from pay phone booths. As Ulasewicz will testify, he had to carry so much change for all the phone calls, his pockets couldn't take it any more, and he had to get himself a bus driver's coin changer. There is also intriguing evidence that Dean may have been paid hush money to Lou Russell, the old spook who'd been minding Heidi's operation at the Columbia Plaza.[102]

In early September, when a bed finally becomes available, Phillip Bailley is ordered to report to St. Elizabeth's—and not just to the general population of the crowded institution, but to the ward for the criminally insane. After two weeks, he is examined by a staff psychiatrist, who pronounces him quite sane.

The strategy, however, has been a success. Bailley, never a strong person to begin with, has been broken. Back in Richey's court, he pleads guilty to a single count in the indictment against him and is sentenced to serve five years in federal prison. He will serve one year before being released. For the rest of his life, Bailley will be dismissed as a nut case,[103] incapable of telling truth from fiction.

In September also, Mo Biner returns from Los Angeles, where she has been spending the summer, meeting new men, and as she puts it in her book, "enjoying myself . . . away from John." After months of agonizing, she says, she had come to the conclusion that "John was not ready to marry me and would not be for some time." So sometime in May or June—or as the usual Watergate cynics point out, about the time the grand jury was meeting on the Bailley case—she quit her job and returned to L.A.

And then one wondrous day, she gets a call from Dean, asking her to marry him. Of course she will. And two weeks later, in a private ceremony[104] at Dean's house in Alexandria, they tie the knot. Present, in addition to the Goldwaters, the Fieldings, and Dean's spymaster John Caulfield, is Heidi Rikan. Heidi, in fact, is one of the bridesmaids.

Leave it once again to Colodny to point out that now that they're married, they can't be compelled to testify against each other in any potential court proceedings. It is, perhaps, ungallant of him to make such a suggestion. To this point, at least, there's been no sign that either might have to testify on anything. Bailley has been shut away and discredited. The burglars have been keeping their mouths shut.

On the other hand, as Dean must know by now, there's no guarantee the cover-up will last forever.

Famous Watergate reporters, Bob Woodward and Carl Bernstein.

Who is Bob Woodward?

Believe it or not, Joe Nesline is in the news again, although not for any crime he may have committed recently.

It's a front-page feature[105] in the *Washington Post*—written, oddly enough, by the paper's budding new Watergate star, Bob Woodward—presenting the aging mobster as a lovable old has-been whose only regret seems to be that you can't find a $20,000 crap game in D.C. any more.

There's been a lull in Watergate coverage lately. The burglars have not yet broken ranks. So maybe Woodward is just casting about for a project.

On the other hand, maybe Nesline is trying to peddle something. Tucked into the tail end of the story is a plug for a prisoner's rights organization called the National Association for Justice that Nesline seems to be championing at the moment. "Nesline gets passionate about prison reform," writes Woodward, "and says that ex-offenders are the most mistreated group in America."

In fact, the National Association for Justice[106] was set up to lobby for the release of Jimmy Hoffa and his return to the presidency of the Teamsters union. Can Woodward be that naïve?

Certainly, none of the revisionists think so. Both Hougan and Colodny, in fact, see Woodward as a de facto intelligence agent.[107] They both point out that the year before he was hired on as a cub reporter for the *Post,* Woodward was an elite naval communications officer, working out of the office of the Chief of Naval Operations in the Pentagon, and conducting briefings for members of the joint chiefs of staff.

Colodny believes that Woodward is carrying water for a military spy ring,[108] under the direction of Admiral Robert Welander, which has also infiltrated the White House at this time. In fact, when Woodward finally does write about the spy ring he fails to mention that Welander is his former commander.

Hougan takes another tack. Wittingly or otherwise, Hougan believes,

Old Gambler

1951 Photo—The Washington Post

dice here is in Monopoly games."

By Bob Woodward
Washington Post Staff Writer

Joe Nesline, 59, has been left behind—an oldtime-gambler who now sits in a chair unconsciously working the air with his hands craving the beloved dice and remembering the days when he was Washington's most prominent crapshooter.

"Gambling, craps and numbers are at their lowest ebb in Washington," Nesline said last week in an interview. "The only dice in Washington is in Monopoly games."

According to some of Nesline's friends and law enforcement officials, this doesn't really mean that gambling in Washington is defunct, just that the days of the $20,000 roll are probably over.

And for Nesline, that is the saddest of occasions. Gambling has been taken over by those who bet on sports, and the crap games have moved to the country clubs in the suburbs, where the big bets are generally only for several hundred dollars.

Those games are friendlier, so there is no need for an honest professional like Nesline to run them for a cut of the winnings, like he did in the old days.

If the days of the high roller are over, at least Nesline still looked the part as he sat in Duke Zeibert's res-

Washington Post, Dec. 23, 1972.

Woodward is channeling information designed to draw attention away from the CIA's involvement in Watergate. He quotes from an internal CIA memo[109] by an officer who writes that his agent, Robert Bennett, head of the Robert R. Mullen Co.—and as such, Howard Hunt's employer—has "been feeding information to Bob Woodward." As the writer goes on to say, Woodward "is suitably grateful for the fine stories and by-lines."

If, indeed, the CIA memo writer is not making this up, it casts a new light on the hubbub that arose when a recent biography of Ben Bradlee, Woodward's editor at the *Post*, quoted Bradlee as saying he never had believed in all this Deep Throat stuff anyway. Woodward, of course, counter-attacked vigorously,[110] but when the dust had settled, the quote was still standing.

David Obst, the agent for Woodward and Bernstein's first book, has said for years that Deep Throat was purely a literary invention,[111] added after the first draft of *All the President's Men* to juice it up for the movie.

The only reason this amounts to anything more than a literary catfight is this: If Woodward is lying about Deep Throat, then who is he trying to protect?

Dean testifying before Watergate Committee.

Dean Switches Sides

On March 23, 1973, the cover-up falls apart. The trials for the Watergate defendants are by now over. Hunt and the Miami burglars have pled guilty. Liddy and McCord have been convicted. The presiding judge in the Watergate burglary case, John Sirica, is about to hand down their sentences.

But first he reads from a letter he has just received from McCord, stating that "political pressure has been applied to the defendants to plead guilty and remain silent . . . Perjury occurred during the trial . . . Others involved in the Watergate operation were not identified in the trial."

All hell breaks loose. The Watergate grand jury is reconvened. The newly formed Senate Watergate Committee roars into action. Before the month is out, Dean is talking with the prosecutor, bargaining for immunity. It doesn't take long for the lawyers in the prosecutor's office to realize that Dean isn't telling the truth about everything. In fact, as one staff member would write, they note "significant discrepancies"[112] in the story Dean is telling them. However, they're willing to cut him some slack. As the first member of the administration to break ranks, he's a particularly valuable witness.

Dean soon becomes the Watergate Committee's star witness—a hero in the press, as well—testifying on national T.V. to the crimes of the Nixon administration. It is a truly impressive performance, well rehearsed and carefully staged. For the occasion, Dean also abandons his contact lenses for the more serious-looking horn-rimmed glasses. Those old enough to have watched his riveting testimony will also remember his adoring wife, Mo Dean, her once flowing blond hair now drawn back in a severe bun, sitting in the gallery behind him.

In the day room at Danbury Federal Prison, Bailley is occasionally able to get a glimpse of the ongoing T.V. spectacular. Until this time, he has had no reason to suspect that his own case is in any way connected with the Watergate scandal now erupting in Washington. He still doesn't know what to make of it.

Despite the new hairdo and the fashionable suits, of course he recognizes the cute blonde sitting a few rows behind Dean. For the first time, he realizes who the nickname in his phone book, "Clout," must refer to.

He remembers thinking: *She could have saved me. If only she had spoken up. She could have explained everything.*

Magruder testifies too. Like Dean, he has also switched sides and is now attempting to shift the responsibility for his own misdeeds on to his superiors. Bailley recognizes him as the man outside "Candy Cane's" apartment that fall day in 1971.

Now, at least he knows who the "boss of bosses" was. But he still doesn't get it. It still doesn't make any sense. Maybe, he thinks, he actually is going crazy.

About this time, Buzzy Patterson, Heidi's ex-husband, finds himself in D.C. for a helicopter association meeting. Although he and Heidi haven't been in touch since their divorce thirteen years ago, he decides to look her up. She's still listed in the phone book under E.L. Rikan, so he gives her a call and the two of them meet for dinner.

Over dinner, Heidi talks excitedly about her important new friends, Mo and John —celebrities now, by virtue of the televised hearings. She parties with them all the time, she says—sometimes at their place in Alexandria, sometimes at her condo in Bethesda.

And it's not just Mo and John, but their friends Barry Goldwater Jr. and his wife Susan. And Senator Lowell Weiker,[113] a member of the Watergate committee. Heidi's in the big time now, just where she always wanted to be.

After dinner, the two of them drive out to Heidi's condo. There she takes out a cigar box filled with pills. She takes a few herself, and offers the box to Patterson. He's not interested, but if that's what she wants, it's not his business.

Then she selects a video from a box under her bed and puts it on the T.V. It's a porno movie. And while that seems more than a little strange after all these years, she is still too beautiful to resist.

He will never see her again.

Nixon, gesturing defiantly as he leaves the White House.

Tricky Dick Leaves Town

To understate matters somewhat, it will not go down as the most successful administration in recent American history.

After pleading guilty to a single count of income tax evasion, stemming from his kick-back days as governor of Maryland, Vice President Spiro Agnew is allowed to resign on October 10, 1973.

Less than a year later, Nixon is out the door, too. Facing certain impeachment and removal from office, he resigns as president on August 8, 1974, the only American president ever to do so.

Die-hard Nixon supporters will argue that the crimes he was accused of were no greater, or certainly no different in kind, than those of his predecessor, Lyndon Johnson[114]—and they may have a point. If it hadn't been for the Watergate break-in—or more precisely, Nixon's attempts, caught on tape, to cover it up—he would probably have served out the remainder of his term. However, once Nixon's enemies—on both the left and the right—see the blood in the water, there's nothing to hold them back.

As part of a deal with the prosecutors, John Dean does four months in prison. When he gets out, he writes a book. Mo writes a book, too. So does Magruder. Everybody, it seems, writes a book. Woodward and Bernstein write several of them, including *All the President's Men,* which is made into a movie starring Robert Redford and Dustin Hoffman.

To date, hundreds of books have been written about Nixon and the Watergate scandal—with only a few of them bothering to question some of the assumptions upon which the popular version of the story is based.

When one of them does—*Silent Coup* by Len Colodny and Robert Gettlin, published in 1991—the Deans sue.[115] Although it isn't the first book to present the call girl theory for the break-in—that distinction belongs to Hougan's *Secret Agenda*—it is the first to link Heidi Rikan to Mo Dean, and thence, of course, to John Dean.

Eventually the case is settled out of court, with both sides claiming victory. There's nothing in the settlement agreement constraining further sales of the book.[116]

In 1997, there's another lawsuit—this time directed at Gordon Liddy, who by now is on the lecture circuit, proclaiming not only that John Dean duped him into the Watergate break-in, but that Dean did so because of Mo's connections to Heidi.

The Deans do not bring the lawsuit themselves, but the lawyers who handled their first lawsuit do. The actual plaintiff is Ida "Maxie" Wells,[117] who will be remembered as the DNC worker on whose desk the burglars had set up their photography equipment in the early morning hours of June 17, 1972. Wells's lawsuit claims that Liddy defamed her by suggesting that she was in any way involved in referring men to the Columbia Plaza call girl operation.

The case would be tried in federal court in Baltimore. The first of what would eventually be two trials ended with the jury hung 7–2 in Liddy's favor. When the judge dismissed the case, Dean's lawyers appealed and were granted a second chance. This time Liddy won unanimously.

The *Washington Post,* which up to this time had been doing a reasonably diligent job of covering the trial, buried the results on a back page of its July 4, 2002 edition, between an article about a man found dead in his car and one about a camp counselor who died in a boating incident.

They didn't respond this time, as they did after the first trial, with an editorial[118] deploring the verdict, which they deemed to be supporting "a 'revisionist'—false would be a better description—account of the scandal."

"The danger of such outcomes as this one," the *Post* continued, "is that this sort of thinking spreads. For whether or not Mr. Liddy's comments legally defamed Ms. Wells, we do know what happened at Watergate—and it had nothing to do with prostitutes."

The editorial is more revealing that it probably intended to be. As should be apparent by now, if anyone tries to tell you he knows everything about Watergate, he either hasn't done his homework or he's trying to sell you a bill of goods.

Where's My Daughter?

For Heidi, Watergate would be a heady time. Dropping in and out of the Deans' Alexandria home, she could feel she was at the center of great events. Sometimes, in order to help the Deans slip away[119] from the press, she would be called upon to chauffeur them around town in her own car.

Kathie, her younger sister, recalls going along on shopping trips with Mo Dean, who wanted just the right new dress for each day of the hearings.

At the height of the scandal, a *Washington Post* gossip columnist would write a lengthy item on the "blond mystery woman"[120] who'd been sitting behind Dean every day at the hearings, noting in passing that Mo had once been the roommate of a "young German woman, whose father was reportedly a Nazi submarine commander." And that—although Heidi's enlisted father obviously received a promotion in the process—was the closest Heidi's name came to surfacing during the Watergate scandal.

In the immediate wake of Watergate, Mo would write a book, talking about her friendship with Heidi. The book even included a glamorous photo of her dear friend, wearing a sable coat—probably the same one she had lent Mo to wear to the White House concert so long ago.

And then, quite suddenly, it was all over. Mo wouldn't speak to her any more. She wouldn't return her calls or letters. Mo—the Deans, we should say—had cut her off.

In a later deposition, Mo would say it was because of Heidi's drinking. The Deans' close friend, Jack Garfield, says it was because John decided it was best to distance themselves from their former friend.

Josephine Alvarez remembers stopping by to visit Heidi in about 1978. Heidi was drinking heavily at the time. Not champagne any more, as she had in the old days, but gin. And when she got drunk enough, she started in on Mo.

"I'm going to get her," Josephine remembers her saying. "I'm going to get her if it's the last thing I do."

It was, of course, an idle threat. By now, as Josephine also recalls, Heidi had split up with Grady Clark and was living with a building contractor.

If Heidi did one thing right, though, it was to arrange for Grady to take care of Kathie. When Kathie graduated from high school, Grady bought her a new Camaro, then supported her while she attended Richland Junior College in Dallas.

While Kathie was going to school, she lived with Grady's son, Grady Jr., and his wife, Cathy. And whenever Heidi, who was apparently still running errands for her friends in D.C., came through Texas, of course Kathie would meet her at the airport.

There was a time, however, as Kathie recalls, that she couldn't make it to the airport. She either couldn't get off work or she had something at school she couldn't get out of—so she asked Cathy to do it for her.

Cathy got there late, though, and Heidi had been sitting in the airport bar for some time. As Cathy would later tell it, she came up behind Heidi and tapped her on the shoulder. Heidi wheeled around to face her, eyes not quite focused and slurring her words. What she said was, "Where's my daughter?"

Retelling the story years later, Kathie says she's not sure what to make of it. The way she sees it, it's not something you can stay up all night worrying about.

The drinking, of course, continued. Kicked out by her latest boyfriend, a mob-connected security consultant in McLean, Virginia, who couldn't take her drinking any longer, Heidi went back to her mother's house in Reading. There was nowhere else to go.

In Reading, she quickly found another sugar daddy—an older guy named Sammy who had a place across town. As a matter of fact, that's where she was when she fell down a flight of stairs and had to be taken, unconscious, to the hospital in an ambulance. At the hospital she regained some measure of consciousness, but was never able to speak again as she lingered for two more weeks.

Kathie, who was working at a new job in Texas, couldn't get there in time before Heidi died. There was no memorial service, and Kathie has no idea what happened to her ashes.

Mo would write—or to be more precise, collaborate with a ghostwriter on—several more books. One of them, a "steamy . . . tale of passion on the Potomac," as *People* magazine would describe it, follows the adventures of a hot little sexpot from the poor part of town who teams up with a slightly older, and much more sophisticated, woman by the name of Echo Bourne. As described in the book, titled *Washington Wives,* Echo is a beautiful, blonde ice maiden who controls a network of women who work for an intelligence operation that specialize in sexual blackmail for political ends.[121]

These days, according to Mo's old friend, Jack Garfield, she spends a lot of time—Garfield thinks maybe too much time—alone in the Deans' home in Beverly Hills. She has, at least, found the life of relative luxury and ease that she longed for as a girl. We can only hope that some day she decides to write another book, because, as the foregoing would indicate, she has at least one more good one in her.

As for Dean, he's fashioned a career for himself as a writer and speaker. He is always in demand for a quote whenever any new Watergate issue crops up. He is currently traveling the country, lecturing on legal ethics.

 ★ ★ ★

Adelheidcharlott Riecken, Heidi, Erika, Kathie Dieter, E.L. Rikan — 1937 to 1990.

ENDNOTES

[1] The most significant Watergate revisionist works are: *Secret Agenda* by Jim Hougan (1984); *Silent Coup* by Len Colodny and Robert Gettlin (1991); *The Strong Man* by James Rosen (2008); *The Secret Plot to Make Ted Kennedy President* by Geoff Shepard (2008).

[2] As reported in the first substantial work on the Watergate scandal, *Nightmare* (1973), by decidedly non-revisionist author J. Anthony Lukas: "So spicy were some of the conversations on the phone [supposedly being monitored in the DNC] that they have given rise to unconfirmed reports that the telephone was being used for some sort of call-girl service catering to congressmen and other prominent Washingtonians." *Nightmare,* p. 201.

[3] In the trial of the Watergate burglars, evidence on the intercepted DNC phone conversations was sealed at the request of an attorney named Charles Morgan. Morgan, who did not represent any of the defendants, made his motion to the court on behalf of the Association of Democratic Chairmen and its employees Spencer Oliver and Ida "Maxie" Wells. It was from Oliver's phone that the calls were supposedly made.

In his motion, Morgan cited a conversation he had had with Watergate prosecutor Earl Silbert, in which Silbert said that one of the arrested burglars, Howard Hunt, "was trying to blackmail Spencer, and I'm going to prove it."

An appeals court accepted Morgan's argument that allowing testimony on the illegal intercepts would be a violation of law. See *Secret Agenda,* pp. 257–60.

[4] There have been two federal court cases over the so-called Revisionist version of Watergate: *Maureen and John Dean v. St. Martin's Press et al.* and *Ida Maxwell Wells v. G. Gordon Liddy.* See Chapter 34.

[5] *Yours in Truth* (2012) by Jeff Himmelman. For a quick summary of the controversy, see "Bob Woodward's desperate damage control," by Alex Pareene at Salon.com, Apr. 30, 2012. Pareene quotes from the book:

"You know I have a little problem with Deep Throat," [Bradlee said] . . . Did that potted [plant] incident ever happen? . . . and meeting in some garage. One meeting in the garage? Fifty meetings in the garage? I don't know how many meetings in the garage. . . . There's a residual fear in my soul that that isn't quite straight."

6

Heidi in uniform, holding Kathie.

[7] "Budding D.C. 'Strip' Tamer than Baltimore's Block." *Washington Post*, Dec. 21, 1961.

[8]

Heidi's business card.

[9] In a letter from Carolyn Rainear to Josephine Alvarez, Jan. 30, 1991.

[10] See: "Organized Crime in Washington" by Frank Browning, *The Washingtonian*, April 1976; "Twilight of a Mobster" by Frank Kuznik, *Regardies,* July 1987*; Masters of Paradise* (1991) by Alan A. Block; *Lucky "325"* (2009) by Josephine Nesline Alvarez.

[11] From an April 1992 interview with Edith Meck by Tony Morris, a retired D.C. intelligence cop then working with private investigator Robert Puglisi for the defense in the *Dean v. St. Martins* case.

[12] In the course of the *Dean vs. St. Martins* case, D.C. gambling figure David McGowan gave a affidavit to defense attorney John Williams, stating that during the late 1960s and though mid-1970, he was acquainted with "a very beautiful woman" named Heidi Rikan, who "would frequent bars and nightclubs in Washington, D.C., and would engage in sexual acts with men in exchange for money." As McGowan went on to state, he was one of those men.

For the complete affidavit, see Appendix on page 182.

[13] Mary Banks, who worked as a maid for Tom Walsh, Heidi's boyfriend in the late 1980s,

said Heidi told her she was a "call girl at the White House." When Mary, who was a very unsophisticated person, asked Heidi to explain, Heidi told her it meant "a lady who meets men and men pay them." Deposition of Mary Banks, Sep. 28, 1993, *Maureen and John Dean v. St Martin's Press et al.*

[14] *Lucky "325"* (2009) by Josephine Nesline Alvarez. Josephine also provided information about Heidi in a number of interviews conducted over the past year. I am extremely grateful for her generosity.

[15] Undercover vice and intelligence cop Carl Shoffler, who will be introduced in this story in Chapter 11. The following exchange is from Shoffler's deposition on Mar. 13, 1995, in *Maureen and John Dean v. St. Martin's Press et al.*

Q. Do you recall what Mae Sullivan told you, if anything, about Heidi Rikan?

A. As I testified earlier, Mae identified her as a Nesline girl.

Q. Meaning what?

A. Meaning that she did Nesline's bidding. Whatever he needed to have done, that she was able to provide the service from carrying a Coke can across the bar to dating someone, to books and records. Her official title at a casino was Bookkeeper . . .

Q. What were her specific accusations about servicing males?

A. That Heidi had sex with a number of football players and that she was able to provide Nesline with inside information.

[16] Donny Anderson, Green Bay Packers; Paul Hornung, Packers and New Orleans Saints; Sonny Jurgenson, Washington Redskins; Eddie Khayat, Redskins; Billy Kilmer, Redskins; Max McGee, Packers; Don Meredith, Dallas Cowboys; Craig Morton, Cowboys; Richie Pettibone, Los Angeles Rams and Redskins; Lance Rentzel, Cowboys; Steve Stonebreaker, Saints; Diron Talbert, Rams and Redskins; Fuzzy Thurston, Packers. Also listed are team owners Clint Murchison, Cowboys; Bedford Wynne, Cowboys; and Art Modell, Cleveland Browns.

[17] A Detroit gambler, Don Dawson, told Moldea "that during the 1950s and 1960s he had been personally involved in the fixing of no fewer than 32 NFL games." *Interference* (1989) by Dan E. Moldea, p. 28.

[18] Moldea relates that a federal investigation into an NFL betting scandal, involving Redskins players and Nesline, was squelched in 1968. Three D.C. gamblers, Richie McCaleb, David McGowan, and Eugene Corsi, "were convicted on conspiracy and racketeering charges and sentenced to prison. Neither Nesline nor any of the Redskins players was charged." An IRS agent would later tell Senate investigators that the case was "fixed." *Interference,* p. 167–171.

[19] As reported by the Associated Press in "Jury Returns 3 Indictments," *The Oregonian*, July, 11, 1968:

"Court records showed subpoenas had been issued for two current Redskin players, quarterback Sonny Jurgensen and guard Vince Promuto…but were with drawn without being served.

"Pro football Commissioner Pete Rozelle said all the players were innocent of any wrongdoing, and court sources stressed they had been called only to give information.

"Indicted were Richard A. McCaleb, 29, and David A. McGowan, 29, both of Alexandria, and Eugene J. Corsi of Washington."

It should be noted that Jurgensen, the Redskins quarterback, as well as two of the bookies, McCaleb and Corsi, are all in Heidi's little black book. For the further adventures of McCaleb and McGowan, in the Washington world of high class prostitution, see the Appendix on page 182.

[20] Heidi's little black book lists a number of D.C. gamblers, including Richie McCaleb, Eugene Corsi, Pete Generis, Lawrence Glass, Nick Katsouros, Alvin Kotz, Larry Levy, Jerry Lilienfeld, Gus Pappas, George Shama, and of course Nesline. Other mob figures include Dick Fincher of Florida and Florence Marcello of the New Orleans crime family. Bill Davis, an American mobster who escaped to Europe in the '60s, is listed at three different addresses in Hamburg, Germany.

[21] According to Josephine, Heidi performed other duties for Nesline while on Antigua. She believes Nesline used Heidi to spy on Gil Beckley, who at the time ran a lay-off operation out of Louisville, Kentucky, and was one of the most important figures in the mob's sports betting business.

However, as Nesline and others in the underworld were aware, Beckley was under federal investigation, and when Beckley and his young girlfriend left on a short cruise, Josephine believes Nesline sent Heidi with them, as a threesome, to spy on Beckley. Obviously, if the feds applied enough pressure to Beckley, he might talk—and if he talked, they'd all be in trouble.

After Beckley was indicted, Josephine says, Nesline ran the lay-offs from his home. She knows because she took the phone calls from high-level gamblers around the country, asking to buy or sell blocks of bets.

While out on bond in February 1970, Beckley disappeared and was presumed murdered, as one prosecutor surmised, "by the top echelon of syndicated organized crime because Beckley might have been cooperating with law-enforcement agencies." *Interference,* p. 223.

[22] Obviously, it's just the tip of an iceberg, but in 1974, as the *Dallas Morning News* would report some years later when he skated on a gambling case also involving the head of the Dallas mob, Joseph Campisi:

"Owens ran into more trouble, but once again he wriggled free with little more than a brief mention in local newspapers. A federal grand jury subpoenaed Owen—along with restaurant owner Joseph Campisi, millionaire builder James L. Williams and two police officers—during an investigation of local bookmaking operations.

"The grand jury had been looking into the Las Vegas-to-Dallas transmission of wagering information. In part, the investigation was prompted by the 1972 discovery of an envelope containing $10,000 during a raid on the home of a known gambler, Bobby Joe Chapman.

"The envelope had the words 'Dallas Cowboys Football Club' written on it. But nothing ever became of the grand jury investigation, and the cash—all in $100 bills—was returned to Chapman."

"SMU booster has lived on edge of limelight," *Dallas Morning News,* Dec. 7, 1986.

[23] Colodny interview with Owen, 1989.

[24] Stage name of Juanita Slusher—prostitute, stripper, and co-star of the groundbreaking 1951 porn movie *Smart Alec.* She was set up by Dallas police for a marijuana bust on October 27, 1957. According to an account of the incident in *Candy Barr* (2008) by Ted Schwarz and Mardi Rustam, Owen was in her apartment at the time of the arrest but not charged. Candy was convicted and sentenced to fifteen years in prison for possession of less than an ounce of marijuana, which had been dropped by her apartment by another stripper shortly before the arrest. While appeals were still under way, she signed up to dance at nightclubs on Hollywood's Sunset Strip, where she made national headlines after she hooked up with celebrity gangster Mickey Cohen. Ordered to prison in 1960, she served three years before being released on parole. While in prison, she was visited by her friend, Dallas club owner Jack Ruby.

[25] Texas connections in Heidi's little black book include Fred Black, LBJ neighbor and friend and business associate of Bobby Baker; Morris Jaffe, LBJ financial advisor; Clint Murchison Jr., principle owner of the Dallas Cowboys; Chito Longoria, developer; Gordon McClendon, radio magnate and friend of Murchison; Ben Barnes, Lt. Governor 1969–73; John White, Texas agriculture commission, 1957–76; Bedford Wynne, co-founder, Dallas Cowboys; Grady Clark, Heidi's sugar-daddy; and John Young, congressman, 1950–76.

[26] In 1972, Clint Murchison's wife Jane informed him that she was getting a divorce. "I can understand a few women here and there, Clint," she reportedly told him, "but thousands of women, no." *The Murchisons* (1989) by Jane Wolfe, p. 335.

[27] Like most successful businessmen at that time in Texas, Clark had good political connections. From 1956–1960, he served as campaign manager and administrative assistant to Texas congressman John Young. In 1976, Young had a sex scandal of his own when

a female staffer went public with allegations that she had received a pay raise after she agreed to have sex with the congressman. The following year, Young's wife committed suicide with a gunshot to her head and Young was defeated for re-election in 1978.

[28] *Mo: A Woman's View of Watergate* (1975) by Maureen Dean and Hays Gorey.

[29] Oddly enough, it's unclear just how Heidi and Mo met. In her book, Mo simply says she met her through George Owen, and doesn't say where. In a 1996 deposition taken in the course of her lawsuit, she is even more vague, or perhaps evasive. She says she met Heidi at some sort of dinner party, but can't remember where, but thinks it was probably Dallas. In the deposition, she makes no mention of Owen's role, but says Heidi was there with Grady Clark. Although she remembers that she and Heidi hit it off right away and even arranged to "meet for tea" the next day, she can't remember any other details. It should also be noted, however, that in her deposition, Mo seems intent on minimizing her friendship with Heidi. Deposition of Maureen Dean, Aug. 28, 1996, *Maureen and John Dean v. St Martin's Press et al.*

[30] Pat, née Patricia Roeder and born in 1937, married football great Paul Hornung in Los Angeles shortly after his team, the Green Bay Packers, won the 1967 Super Bowl. She moved with him to New Orleans when he was dealt in the expansion draft to the Saints later that year, and that is where she and Mo met. At the time, Mo's husband, George Owen, was working for the Saints.

When Pat's marriage to Hornung broke up about a year later, she moved back to Los Angeles, where she had a part in the soap opera "Days of Our Lives" and roomed with Mo. Like Mo, she would also go on to collaborate with ghost writers on novels about party girls living in the fast lane.

The Season (1975), written with Robin Moore, is a soft-core sex romp featuring star NFL quarterback Cal Winston and his beautiful and spirited girlfriend Laura, who, like Pat, had "long chestnut hair shimmering against her shoulders . . . (and) high cheekbones that slanted up to meet emerald-green eyes . . . Her body looked better without clothes, Cal thought, feeling the heat rise in him as he thought of her full breasts, flat stomach, and long legs. There was a hidden, almost secret sexuality about her he was never able to describe."

Pretty Eyes (1980), written with Howard Liss, is about the adventures of a remarkably similar, but somewhat older woman caught up in the Hollywood rat race. Her name is Liz, and at one point in the proceedings, she observes: "I'm the best-looking 47-year-old in this town, because I exercise, I watch my diet, I keep busy, and I get laid every night." Pat Hornung died, alone and destitute, in Pompano Beach, Florida, in 2003. According to family members, she had been defrauded of the settlement she'd received in the divorce from her latest husband and didn't even have money to pay her electric bill. Shortly before her death, her brothers had to travel to Pompano Beach to pay her debts and get the electricity turned back on. Not much later, family members suspect, she was murdered for her life insurance. However, they never made a complaint to the police, and the case was never investigated.

[31] Celebrity dentist Jack Garfield, now in his early 70s and living in Palm Springs, Calif., has been an invaluable resource for this book. Not only did he date Mo when she was rooming with Pat Hornung in Los Angeles, but after she married Dean, he became good friends with John, as well.

In the spring of 1973, while Dean would have been working out the details of his arrangement with the Watergate prosecutor's office, Garfield took Mo and Heidi to Miami for a short vacation at the Palm Bay Club. After Dean was released from prison, the Deans lived for a while at his house in Bel Air, during which time he recalls driving Dean to the plastic surgeon to have a hair transplant. "I think he had his eyes done, too," says Garfield. Garfield is also close to Dean's prep school roommate, former Congressman Barry Goldwater Jr., who lived at his house from 1976–82.

Mo at the Watergate hearings, 1973.

[33] In his generally excellent biography of Nixon, *The Arrogance of Power,* Anthony Summers writes that Mickey Cohen gave Nixon $5,000 (roughly $50,000 in today's money) for his 1948 House campaign and another $75,000 (three-quarters of a million dollars today) for his 1950 Senate race. The Senate contribution was arranged by calling together about 250 of the top West Coast mobsters for a dinner in the banquet room of the Hollywood Knickerbocker Hotel. At the end of the evening, Cohen ordered the doors locked until the desired figure was obtained.

"Mickey Cohen's support operation on Nixon's behalf was no philanthropic initiative undertaken by Cohen alone," writes Summers. "The order came, he made clear in his memoir, from 'the proper persons back East.' The 'proper persons,' he explained, were Frank Costello and Meyer Lansky, the men who founded the national syndicate, the emperors of organized crime." *The Arrogance of Power* (2000) by Anthony Summers, pp. 54–57.

Summers goes on to report that in 1960 the mob gave Nixon $1 million—half of it coming from New Orleans mafia boss Carlos Marcello and the other half from Chicago boss Sam Giancana. *The Arrogance of Power,* p. 213.

[34] "When Richard Nixon was president," writes Don Fulsom in his recent book, *Nixon's Darkest Secrets,* "a disreputable character named Charles Gregory 'Bebe' Rebozo (a.k.a Charles Gregory) all but lived in the White House. Not known beyond the executive mansion at that time—or to most people even now—Rebozo had working and sleeping quarters there . . .

"In fact, the only government entity that knew much about Bebe was the FBI, which said he was cozy with Mafia biggies, especially Tampa godfather Santos Trafficante and Alfred 'Big Al' Polizzi of Cleveland. Big Al was a drug trafficker associated with the Syndicate's financial genius Meyer Lansky . . .

"The thirty-seventh president's intimate relationship with a mafia crony like Rebozo raises serious questions about just how deeply the country's biggest and most profitable illegal business—the blood-soaked Mob—had gotten its sinister hooks into Nixon.

"In the 1960s, crooked gambling operations alone brought in an estimated $500 billion a year." *Nixon's Darkest Secrets* (2012) by Don Fulsom, chapter 4.

[35] In addition to an estimated $1 million dollars contributed to Nixon's 1972 re-election campaign, the Teamsters gave another $500,000 to Nixon personally. The pay-off was negotiated with the Teamster officials who had taken over the union's leadership while Hoffa was in prison. Under the terms of his release from prison, Hoffa was barred from holding union office for a period of ten years. *Arrogance of Power,* p. 399.

[36] See *A Heartbeat Away* (1974) by Richard M. Cohen and Jules Whitcover.

[37] Based on the author's 1986 interviews with Carl Shoffler, as well as notes on Shoffler's

own records of the Pat Adams investigation, which were made by Shoffler's friend, author Dan Moldea. Also, recent interviews with Pat Adams' younger sister, Cynthia Rodriguez.

[38] Twenty-eight-year-old call girl Pat Adams left her apartment on February 6, 1969, in the company of her boyfriend, Donald Brew, and was never seen again. Although Brew was, of course, considered a suspect in her disappearance, Pat's body was never found and her disappearance was classified as a missing persons case. Shoffler, who soon became aware of the rumors that Pat Adams had been trying to blackmail Agnew, thought it was likely that she'd been murdered.

In 2007, Brew, then in failing health, turned himself in to authorities and confessed to murdering Pat Adams, but did so without implicating Nesline. Although Brew said he buried her in Prince Williams County, Va., authorities were never able to find the body, leading to speculation that he may have told less than the full truth in exchange for medical care. Nevertheless, Brew was convicted of the murder, and he died in a Virginia prison the following year. For a fairly oblivious account of Brew's confession, see the *Washington Post,* Mar. 11, 2007.

[39] See *Official and Confidential, The Secret Life of J. Edgar Hoover* (1993) by Anthony Summers, p. 53:

"Edgar's vast filing system was part of his stock in trade. He was proud of it, just as he was proud of his scientific advances. Presidents and politicians, however, had to live with the threat—real or imagined—that those files could bring disaster down on their heads. . . . Edgar's record system included files with names like the OBSCENE file, the SEX DEVIATE program, COINTEL, OFFICIAL AND CONFIDENTIAL, PERSONAL AND CONFIDENTIAL . . . He created this private fiefdom in such a way that—as long as he lived—he had absolute power over those who served him, and the weapons to fend off those who did not."

[40] "Through field offices scattered around the country, the Office of Security maintains close ties with state and local police. In each field office, a 'black book' is kept of the males and females who can be safely recruited to entertain the CIA's visitors. The black books contain names, telephone numbers and details, gleaned largely from local vice squads. In Washington, for example, CIA agents paid regular visits to photograph documents."

"The CIA's Sex Squad," by columnists Jack Anderson and Les Whitten, *Washington Post,* June 22, 1976.

[41] "Among those visitors whom the CIA had occasion to entertain," writes Jim Hougan in *Secret Agenda,* "were foreign leaders, agents in transit and defectors. But entertainment was by no means the only purpose served by the agency's liaison with local vice squads around the country. Blackmail was another function, and, toward that end, the Office of Security maintained safe houses—literally, houses or apartments untraceable to the

CIA—in a number of American cities . . .

"In New York and San Francisco for example, CIA agent George White installed prostitutes in lavish apartments outfitted with two-way mirrors, video equipment and microphones . . . and CIA operatives—both thoughtful physicians and hardened agents, such as Colonel White—could sit in secret rooms (equipped with chamber pots) and watch the fun through two-way mirrors . . . " *Secret Agenda* by Jim Hougan, pp. 14–15.

[42] Rothstein, who served as a detective with the NYPD from 1965 to 1980, says he was aware of intelligence agency-run sexual blackmail operations in New York City at East 36th and Lexington, East 57th and Third, and East 56th and Second.

[43] "A source for both J. Edgar Hoover's FBI and the CIA under Allen Dulles and Richard Helms," writes Hougan, "Captain Blick maintained exhaustive files on the subject of sexual deviance, files said to have included the names of every prostitute, madam, pimp, homosexual, pederast, sado-masochist, and most points in between, of whatever nationality, who came to the attention of the police in the country's capital." *Secret Agenda,* p. 13–14.

[44] In her Watergate memoir, Mo says she and John were unable to get together over Christmas because, although John didn't admit it till later, he was spending time with his estranged wife, Karla. "But there was some good news. He would visit me in Los Angeles for New Year's. Well, I wanted him for both holidays, but I consoled myself with the half-loaf." *Mo,* p. 47.

What Mo neglects to say is that she apparently also consoled herself by spending the Christmas vacation with Heidi in Miami. Josephine Alvarez, who was living in Miami at the time, remembers the visit quite clearly. She was staying at the Fountainbleu, and Heidi and Mo were at the Palm Bay Club, which was then one of Miami's hot spots.

As it happened, the Palm Bay Club was also the home base for another of John Dean's Staunton Military Academy friends, Lance Cooper. Cooper was the Palm Bay Club's golf pro and all-around social organizer.

[45] Deposition of Carl Shoffler Mar. 13, 1995, *Maureen and John Dean v. St. Martin's Press et al.*

[46] This revealing little story comes from Len Colodny's tape-recorded 1989 interview with George Owen, the mob-connected Dallas club owner, who was, of course, Heidi's former boyfriend as well as Mo Dean's ex-husband. Here's Owen:

"Let me tell you, about 19 . . . fuck, I can't even remember what day it was. It was the day Hoffa got out of jail. I got a call from a very influential man in Washington, D.C., who was a friend of Clint's, who said I have got to talk with you."

Clint, of course, is Owen's millionaire friend Clint Murchison Jr., owner of the Dallas Cowboys. Clint's influential friend in Washington is undoubtedly the lobbyist Irving

Davidson, who represented Murchison's interests as well as those of New Orleans mobster Carlos Marcello. At the time, Irving—whose name, it should be noted, appears in Heidi's second little black book—was active in the effort to get Hoffa out of prison.

Owen continues:

"I said, oh fuck, I ain't coming up there, why do I want to come to Washington for? You come down here. He said, nope, this is important and I need to talk to you, it's life or death. So I got on a plane and went up there and I said what the fuck do you want. He says Hoffa is getting out of jail. Now these people, John Dean, and, ah, Nixon are the only two votes, and Mitchell had a vote, to let Hoffa come back into the union or whatever the fuck he's in."

As usual, the garrulous Owen doesn't have all the details nailed down, but he's obviously talking about the controversy within the administration over whether Hoffa, once he's released from prison, should be allowed to return to the Teamster's presidency. Part of Dean's job as presidential counsel was to sign off on presidential pardons, and whether Owen and his mob friends had an exaggerated view of Dean's importance in the process is open to question.

"So anyway," says Owen, "Mitchell is agreed to let him come back in. The other two have not responded. You've got to talk to John Dean. I said, what the fuck are you talking about . . . I don't care anything about talking to him. He and I are not even speaking. I never met him. He says, I can't help it, you've got to do it. I said the only way I know how to do it is talk to Heidi. He said, well, that's what you've got to do. So I called Heidi and talked to her and told her what I wanted and all that crap."

According to Owen, Heidi carries the message to Dean. It's unclear from the interview what the message was or how it may have affected the terms of Hoffa's parole. However, it is worth noting that according to Hoffa's lawyer, Benton Becker, Hoffa always blamed Dean for the provision in his parole that prevented him from returning to the Teamsters.

See also: "Nixon's Hoffa Pardon Has An Odor," by James Warren, *Chicago Tribune,* April 8, 2001.

[47] The best summary of Dean's checkered past comes from Geoffrey Shepard, author of *The Secret Plot to Make Ted Kennedy President,* which, despite its over-the-top title, is an extremely level-headed account of how the Senate Watergate committee and the special prosecutor's office sometimes manipulated the facts in order to achieve their political ends. Shepard got his information on Dean from Dean's official parole records.

"Dean grew up in Marion, Ohio, and first attended Baker High School—switching to Staunton Military Academy in Virginia early in his sophomore year. It is not clear what happened at Baker High, but in that era you got sent away to military school only if you came from a military family or there was trouble on the home front.

"He graduated from Staunton in 1957, but did not go into the military. Instead, he enrolled at Colgate University in New York, intending to major in English. Things did not go well for him at Colgate and he again switched schools in the middle of his sophomore year—returning to Ohio to attend tiny Wooster College, where his activities centered on the Pre-Law Club.

"In his senior year, Dean married Karla Hennings, daughter of Senator Thomas Henning of Missouri. He graduated in the lower third of this class in 1961, but did not go to law school. Instead, he enrolled in American University in Washington, D.C., doing graduate work in political science.

"In 1962, he dropped out of American University to enroll in Georgetown Law School, from which he graduated in 1965.

"His first (and only) experience in private practice was with the small communications law firm of Welsh & Morgan, who specialized in obtaining very lucrative FCC broadcast licenses. Dean was fired in six months 'for unethical conduct': Apparently, while working on a license application for a firm client, he also prepared an application on behalf of his mother-in-law in St. Louis. It is not clear from the records whether the Dean application was in direct competition with the one he was working on for the firm or just one that would have reduced the scarce number of such licenses . . .

"Dean quickly became Minority Counsel to the House Judiciary Committee, courtesy of Rep. Bill McCullough of Ohio—and Wooster College alum. For reasons that remain unclear, Dean 'was terminated effected August 13, 1967' and remained unemployed for the next six months.

"In February of 1968, Dean became Associate Director of the Commission to Reform the Federal Criminal Laws . . . While on the Commission staff, Dean obtained a letter from his previous law firm that qualified his termination, saying it 'resulted from a basic disagreement over law firm policies regarding the nature and scope of an associate's activities'—but the letter notably did not rescind the prior characterization of being terminated for unethical conduct."

From "Troublesome Facts About John Dean," by Geoff Shepard at thenewnixon. org/2009/11/11.

[48] See *Silent Coup*, p. 112. Robert T. Hartmann, one of Dean's fellow staffers on Capitol Hill and later a top aide to Gerald Ford, is the source of the quote about the "arm's length attitude" toward Dean.

"Another Dean strategy, frequently in evidence before he reached the White House," write Colodny and Gettlin, "was a propensity for unauthorized use of his superior's name. 'Either [Dean] would just lie about it,' said this former Dean colleague, who prefers anonymity, 'or he would mention something obliquely to the person whose name he was going to use and would do it in such a way that the guy wouldn't notice Dean was going to extrapolate authority from it. It's an old trick in Washington.'"

[49] In his own Watergate memoir, *Blind Ambition,* Dean writes about an earlier assignment from Nixon's chief of staff, H.R. Haldeman, in January 1971, to investigate suspected ties between billionaire Howard Hughes and chairman of the Democratic National

Committee Larry O'Brien. Although Dean's investigation went nowhere, Nixon's people later found out through the IRS that O'Brien was at one time on $160,000 retainer to Hughes. See *Blind Ambition* by John Dean, pp. 56–58. Also *Silent Coup*, p. 102.

Dean has at various times attempted to distance himself from his own book, which was written with the help of noted author Taylor Branch, saying that he didn't bother to read the text before it was published. Branch and his editor Alice Mayhew both dispute this—raising the question in some minds about why Dean would now try to deny his own words. Revisionist historians like Colodny view the aborted Hughes assignment as the cover that Dean used more than a year later to order the Watergate break-ins. For more on this controversy, see Colodny's website at Watergate.com.

[50] "In the spring of 1971, Caulfield had begun to think about leaving the White House in order to set up the private security business . . . He wrote up his suggestions in a memo for John Dean, suggesting $500,000 to fund what he called Operation Sandwedge . . .

"Caulfield told us that Sandwedge was 'my initiative, but it really involved a lot of discussions with John Dean . . . '" *Silent Coup*, pp. 107–8.

[51] "Dean soon devised a project to help him get his foot in the door. On August 16, 1971, he produced a memorandum titled 'Dealing with our Political Enemies' . . . Dean suggested that key White House staff members collect names of administration opponents whom 'we should be giving a hard time' and then used various government departments and agencies to 'screw them.' This Dean memo was the germ that led to a White House 'enemies list.'" *Silent Coup*, p. 104.

[52] Bailley's law practice, it should also be noted, included more than just defending streetwalkers. He made the *Washington Post* in a story headlined "Acquittal in Sex Case a Hollow Victory," when he won the acquittal of a 28-year-old man arrested for soliciting an undercover policewoman for sex. The court victory was a hollow one, as the news story explained, because the arrest had already cost the man his job and wrecked his marriage.

"The case," reported the *Post*, "involved the latest in a series of trials arising from the Washington police department's policy of deploying policewomen in downtown street corners to apprehend men—most of them from the suburbs—who are looking for prostitutes."

Bailley contended that the use of the policewoman constituted "entrapment."

"After first asking twice if she would like a ride 'downtown' and hearing her say 'no,' Miss Mann [the undercover policewoman] said the man asked her 'if we could do something.'

"She testified that she answered 'What do you mean?' He replied 'Can I get a (act of oral sodomy)?'"

"Judge Tim C. Murphy granted the acquittal sought by Bailley on grounds that oral sodomy is not covered in the term prostitution." *Washington Post*, July 31, 1970.

[53] Those who have been following this controversy over the years will find it highly significant that both Josephine and Heidi's sister Kathie have a distinct memory of Heidi using the name. Until now, opponents of the call-girl theory have tried to argue that the name Kathie Dieter was nothing more than an invention of the much-maligned Phillip Bailley.

[54] Jeannine, who now runs a community health clinic in Florida, was an Air Force lieutenant and nurse in 1993 when she was deposed for the Deans' lawsuit.

As her brother Phil Bailley's secretary, she testified, she kept records of calls to the law office. She was in the process of consolidating the numbers from her office book and Bailley's book into a third book on the day the FBI raided the office.

Under questioning, she said she remembered a number of names and code names of persons calling about the DNC and the Columbia Plaza operation, including Kathie Dieter and Mo Biner, or "Clout," as Jeannine also had her listed.

Q. Now, were you able to associate any of the nicknames with the actual names that I asked you about before?

A. Yes . . .

Q. And what name did you put with Clout?

A. Mo Biner.

Q. And why was it that you remember that nickname and Mo Biner?

A. Because at the time I was seventeen years old. I did not know what the word "clout" meant. It was next to her name on the right-hand side. And I went to my brother at the end of the day or sometime shortly thereafter and asked him what "clout" meant. He explained it to me and then I said, oh well, I put it in the left-hand margins over here in this book and he said that was fine . . .

Q. Okay. What did he tell you "Clout" meant?

A. He said that she had political connections and that she was an important person.

Deposition of Jeannine Bailley, Sep. 29, 1993, *Gordon Liddy v. John Dean* and *Maureen and John Dean v. St Martin's Press et al.*

[55] Aug. 29, 1996, *Maureen and John Dean v. St. Martin's Press et al.*

[56] "Cleanup Asked in Staff of Velde Group," by Murray Marder, *Washington Post,* Jan. 21, 1954.

[57] Bob Smith, who worked at Fensterwald's Committee to Investigate Assassinations, told author Jim Hougan that "Russell regaled him with anecdotes about intimate conversations between prostitutes and the politicians at the DNC." As Hougan also reports, "The private eye also bragged to Fensterwald and told another investigator, former Treasury agent Kennard Smith, that he was tape-recording conversations between Columbia Plaza prostitutes and their clients." *Secret Agenda,* p. 118.

[58] See Hougan's discussion of CIA contract agent Lee R. Pennington's destruction of Mc-Cord's files after the Watergate arrests. "Internal CIA documents," writes Hougan, "make reference to the fact that Pennington repeatedly briefed his case officer on McCord's situation vis-à-vis Watergate, and that Pennington provided the [Office of Security's] Security Research Staff with investigative reports about Jack Anderson that McCord had prepared on the basis of Lou Russell's information. It appears, then, that Lee R. Pennington was McCord's cut-out to the Security Research staff." *Secret Agenda,* p.234.

[59] See for example, "Church Probers Find 'Gaps' in CIA Records" by George Lardner Jr., *Washington Post,* May 17:

"Chairman Frank Church (D-Idaho) said the committee has not come up with an explanation for the missing documents concerning secret CIA operations, but plans to pursue the issue with agency officials . . .

"Former CIA Director Richard Helms, it was learned last year, ordered the destruction of various tape records of conversations in his office. The destruction was ordered shortly before Helms resigned as CIA director in January 1973.

"The CIA maintained it was a routine destruction of unnecessary record, but Sen. H. Howard Baker Jr. (R-Tenn), a member of the Senate Watergate committee and the Church committee, contested the claim and said that the telephone conversations with former President Nixon and top White House officials were apparently among the recordings that were destroyed.

"The destruction occurred a week after Senate Majority Leader Mike Mansfield (Mont.) wrote Helms to ask that any Watergate-related evidence be retained."

[60] The identity of Chrissie, which is how she was known to Bailley, remains a puzzle. Bailley says Heidi (who, of course, he knew as Kathie Dieter) first brought up her name when she showed him a photo of herself, Mo, and a woman she called Chrissie, posing on a beach at Lake Tahoe. "They'll be joining us," Bailley remembers her saying.

[61] As Dean writes, he received word that a confidential informant for the Knapp Commission, then investigating police corruption in New York City, had "wired the lush business quarters of a madam named Xavier Hollander and made tapes of famous clients 'having intercourse and engaging in abnormal sexual practices.'" The informant, a Teddy Ratenoff, "had also managed to copy Ms. Hollander's address book. But there was *another* address book, for sensitive political people, and it was not known whether Ratenoff had it." In the end, he decided that the "information cut such a wide political swath there was little chance of its being put to political use." He did, however, think it would "be entertaining to drop hints of the information" around the White House and "let people know that the counsel's office had ears in hidden corners." . . . *Blind Ambition,* pp. 29–30.

[62] When Dean testified before the Senate Watergate Committee in 1973, he said that he

barely knew Ulasewicz. In his book *Blind Ambition,* he tries to maintain some distance as well, claiming that he only knew that one of Caulfield's operatives was named Tony. Obviously, though, unless Ulasewicz is fantasizing his meeting with Dean, Dean is once again lying. Ulasewicz's description of this meeting with Dean appears on page 242 of his memoir, *The President's Private Eye.* As Caulfield, Ulasewicz's boss, would tell the authors of *Silent Coup* when they asked him about it: "He's full of shit when he says he knew very little about Ulasewicz." *Silent Coup,* pp.101–105.

[63] "Since the demise of Caulfield's proposed Operation Sandwedge, Dean had been searching for a way to undertake the gathering of political intelligence. Magruder reported in his book [*An American Life*] that when he approached Dean about finding a lawyer for the CRP, Dean said, 'Maybe we could combine an intelligence job with the general counsel . . . I'll check into it.'" *Silent Coup,* p. 119.

[64] For this and all subsequent Gemstone meetings, the best source is G. Gordon Liddy's 1980 Watergate memoir, *Will.* Liddy may be quite eccentric, but of all the White House figures in this story, he seems to be the most consistently honest. He is also a pretty good writer. It should be noted that when he wrote the book, Liddy had not yet realized how deeply he had been duped. *Will,* pp. 251–52.

[65] Of all the White House figures in this story, Magruder seems to be the one least suited for life in the shark tank. After serving seven months in prison for his role in the Watergate break-in, he became a Presbyterian minister, serving in Louisville, Kentucky, and Columbus, Ohio.

In 2003, Magruder was arrested in Columbus after he passed out intoxicated on a sidewalk. He eventually pleaded guilty to disorderly conduct. In 2007 he was charged after causing two collisions on an Ohio highway, then slamming his own car into a concrete divider. He eventually pleaded guilty to a charge of operating a vehicle in a reckless manner. "Watergate figure charged in Rt. 315 collisions," *Columbus Dispatch,* July 26, 2007.

Since Watergate, he has repeatedly changed his story, sometimes implicating John Mitchell in the break-ins, and on other occasions admitting the role he and John Dean played. The best summary of Magruder's many stories, which is to be found in *The Strong Man* by James Rosen, includes the following exchange from Magruder's deposition in the *Dean v. St. Martins* lawsuit:

Q. Is it true that John Dean was one of the people in the White House that was pushing for the Gemstone plan?

A. Yes.

Q. Is it, in fact, truthful that you and John Dean had prior knowledge of the Watergate break-in?

A. Yes.

The Strong Man, p. 294.

[66] Nixon's top advance man, Ron Walker, told author Anthony Summers that he was aware of the brothel next to the DNC. "I knew it from the Advance Office," he said. "I had colleagues that used call girl rings." According to another longtime aide who spoke to Summers on condition of anonymity, one of those colleagues, deputy protocol chief Nick Ruwe "was always using those call girls at the place next to the DNC." *Arrogance of Power,* p. 422.

[67] Most Watergate books do an exhaustive job on Gemstone, but as usual, Liddy's account is best. He doesn't spare anyone, including himself. *Will*, pp. 271–76.

[68] The charts, as the oblivious Liddy notes in his own book, were prepared by graphic artists at the CIA:
   "Hunt and I finally had our plans made in fullest detail. I told him of the need for a cash flowchart and that I'd like to have our diagrams also put in chart form for my presentation to the Attorney General . . . Hunt was up to the challenge. He took our own crude but legible diagrams to professionals: the CIA." *Will*, p. 267.

[69] For Ulasewicz's detailed account, see *The President's Private Eye,* p. 246. For a discussion of Dean's denial, see *Silent Coup,* p. 131.

[70] *Will*, p. 280. *Blind Ambition*, p. 74.

[71] When Liddy wrote *Will* (see pp. 225–233), he was still unaware of how badly he had been duped on the break-in at the office of Ellsburg's psychiatrist. His reporting is so good, however, that it is possible to see what he himself missed at the time. As usual, when it comes to intelligence shenanigans, Hougan's *Secret Agenda* is best. In a chapter entitled "The Unplumbed Depths of Daniel Ellsburg," pp. 41–56, he makes the case that, unknown to Liddy, of course, Howard Hunt was sending regular dispatches to his bosses at CIA headquarters.

[72] James Rosen says it best: "Faced with mounting evidence that officials in the White House and CRP had set up their own covert operations unit, with Liddy the central player, CIA acted as any intelligence agency would. After all, permitting Liddy's little unit to operate unchecked, targeting anything and anybody in Washington, utterly beyond the watch of influence of the nation's premier spy agency, would have violated every known principle of bureaucratic behavior, and the spy game especially." *Strong Man*, p. 282.

[73] See *Will,* p. 286.

[74] Magruder will later claim that Mitchell gave final approval of the Gemstone plan at a March 30 meeting in Key Biscayne, Florida. Dean and Liddy were not present at the meeting, and except for Magruder, those who were there agree that Mitchell did not do

so. See Rosen's *Strong Man,* pp. 270–73 for a good summary of Magruder's changing stories on this point.

[75] Deposition of John E. Rudy, June 19, 1996, *Maureen and John Dean v. St Martin's Press et al.*

[76] *Secret Agenda,* p. 114.

[77] Author's interview with Rudy, Sept. 25, 1986.

[78] *Secret Agenda,* p. 118.

[79] Rudy deposition, June 19, 1996. Also, as Hougan writes in *Secret Agenda,* p. 119:

"Rudy says that while Russell's information was accurate, it was apparent that Russell was trying to divert him from the Bailley case and from the Columbia Plaza. As we shall see, that effort would prove unnecessary: the Justice Department would bring pressure upon Rudy to turn his attention 'to more important things,' and the judge who was to try the case, Nixon appointee Charles Richey, would all but order the litigants to settle the case in chambers."

[80] See *Will,* p. 325.

[81] *Secret Agenda,* p. 145.

[82] As Hougan argues, the real problem may have been that, in fact, no bugs were ever planted in the DNC. It seems that McCord was lying about that, too. Despite a thorough search after the arrests, the FBI never did find a bug in the DNC. A telephone bug reported by a DNC employee in September, more than two months after the break-in, was surely a phony. See *Secret Agenda,* p. 244.

So the question is: if there never was a bug in the DNC, then what were McCord and his assistant who was monitoring the transmissions, Alfred Baldwin, listening to? Hougan suggests that given the FBI's failure to find a bug and Baldwin's assertion that the eavesdropping began before the break-in took place, the only logical conclusion is that McCord was monitoring Heidi's Columbia Plaza operation.

[83] *Evening Star,* June 9, 1972. See also "Philip & Astrid & Etc.," *Time,* June 26, 1972.

[84] Bailley's indictment, *U.S. v. Philip M. Bailley*, No. 1190–72, does not name any of the alleged victims. An FBI document dated May 18, 1972, does. There were six of them. By comparing the charges in the indictment to the FBI's list, it is now possible to say with certainty that none of the alleged victims was associated with the Columbia Plaza.

[85] "I recall a couple of assistant United States attorneys coming to my office in connection with a newspaper story claiming that a lawyer, or secretary, from the White House was allegedly connected with a call girl ring. As I recall, we had trouble figuring out who, if anyone, at the White House was involved. But I never made a copy of an address book." *Conservatives Without Conscience* (2006) by John Dean, p. xvii.

This is John Dean at his finest. First he sidesteps the question of who invited Rudy and Smith to his office, implying—although he called them and sent a limo to pick them up—that they were the ones interested in finding out if anyone at the White House was involved. Then he says he never made a copy of an address book—which, as it happens, is actually correct. He had a secretary do it.

[86] Tape-recorded interview by Colodny, Apr. 28, 1989. *Silent Coup,* p. 133.

[87] We know that Roemer McPhee was a back-channel to Judge Richey because, for starters, Dean was recorded on the White House taping system telling Nixon that McPhee was being used as a go-between with Richey on the Democratic civil suit against the CRP, over which Richey also presided. *White House transcripts,* Sept. 15, 1972.

Oddly enough, Dean actually testified that this was so before the Watergate committee. The following is from *All the President's Men* by Woodward and Bernstein, p. 206:

"Dean, Mitchell, and Haldeman all later testified that a Washington lawyer, Roemer McPhee, had engaged in private discussions about the civil case with Judge Richey. Dean testified that McPhee initiated private discussions with the judge to seek favorable treatment for the administration in the civil suit." This is considered *ex parte* contact, and is illegal. Obviously, Dean never intended for anyone to apply this helpful insight to his dealings with McPhee on June 9, 1972.

[88] *Will,* p. 327. Obviously, the nature of the mission had changed.

[89] All quoted dialogue is from the official transcript of Bailley's June 15 hearing in U.S. District Court for the District of Columbia, Criminal Case No. 1190–72.

[90] See "Richey May Get U.S. Judgeship," *Baltimore Sun,* Mar. 5, 1971. "Charles R. Richey, general counsel for the Maryland Public Service Commission, is expected to be named shortly to a seat on the federal district court here. Mr. Richey, 46, who reportedly is a close friend of Vice President Agnew, would replace Chief Judge Edward M. Curran, who is expected to retire shortly."

[91] "According to the logs maintained by the Watergate's private security service, General Security Service, Inc., McCord, under an alias, signed in at 10:50 p.m. He took the elevator to the eighth floor, his announced destination." *Silent Coup,* p. 155.

[92] For a detailed account of the second break-in, see the appropriate chapters in *Secret Agenda.* Hougan, with his brilliant deconstruction, was the first to focus on McCord's and Lou Russell's strange behavior that night.

[93] Once again, the best source is *Secret Agenda.* For Russell's remark to his daughter about having to do some work for McCord that night, see *Secret Agenda,* p. 192.

[94] As recently released documents show, the phone used by Maxie Wells was indeed the target of the wiretaps—not Larry O'Brien's. As reported by Jeff Stein in his online column for *AND Magazine* on July 16, 2013, shortly after the long-sealed documents based on the burglars' wiretap notes were made public:

"O'Brien's name is not on the list of the bugging targets released Monday by the National Archives and Records Administration, on order of Chief Judge Royce Lamberth of the U.S. District Court for the District of Columbia. And that throws a wrench into the generally accepted answer to the affair's central question: What were the burglars doing in the Watergate?…

"A contending theory…has long posited that neither O'Brien nor the Democrats' political and financial secrets were the plumbers' targets: They were after another phone at DNC headquarters, which was allegedly being used to set up dates with prostitutes for visiting out-of-town Democratic officials.

"That phone belonged to DNC official R. Spencer Oliver, who was often away on business, according to those accounts. In his absence, they say, it was used by Oliver's secretary, Ida Wells, to set up dates with hookers for prominent Democrats visiting town.

"Tuesday's release revealed that the name of Oliver and Wells were on the bugging targets list, compiled by the White House plumbers' wiretapper, Alfred Baldwin, and promptly sealed for 40 years—until now."

[95] Deposition of Carl Shoffler Mar. 13, 1995, *Maureen and John Dean v. St. Martin's Press et al.* See also *Secret Agenda,* pp. 320–323—although at the time he wrote the book, Hougan seemed willing to give Shoffler a pass, seeing him as a "much maligned cop, a lint trap for ultimately senseless suspicions."

[96] The snitch, Robert Merritt, recently wrote an as-told-to book entitled *Watergate Exposed,* in which he claims to be the one who tipped off Shoffler about the Watergate break-in. And while Merritt's claim on this crucial matter is dubious, many elements of his story appear to be true.

Merritt says he got the word about an imminent break-in at the Watergate from a transvestite friend of his who operated the switchboard at the Columbia Plaza. While some of the detail of Merritt's story about the switchboard operator's warning just don't make sense, it appears that in fact Shoffler had an informant who ran the telephone switchboard at the Columbia Plaza. That is substantiated by Shoffler's friend and former partner on D.C. intelligence, Karl Milligan.

Documents show that Merritt was a long-time snitch for Shoffler, infiltrating radical groups in D.C. After the Watergate arrests, Shoffler encouraged Merritt to establish a liaison with the first lawyer for the Watergate burglars, Douglas Caddy, because both Merritt and Caddy were homosexual. Caddy, as it happened, was employed by Mullen and Co., the same CIA front organization that Howard Hunt worked for after his supposed resignation from the Agency. Caddy, it should be noted, is also Merritt's co-author on *Watergate Exposed,* and if you can figure that one out, you're better than I am.

[97] The two are Karl Milligan and Robert Puglisi, both of whom went on to start successful private investigative firms in the D.C. area. Over the course of both Dean-inspired lawsuits, they were hired as investigators for the defense—in which capacity they worked closely with Shoffler, who encouraged them and gave them tips. Over the years, they say, whenever they asked him how he happened to be waiting outside the Watergate on the night of the burglary, he would just give them a wink and a smile. Milligan, in particular, has made a point of trying to figure out what Shoffler was actually up to on the night of the Watergate arrests.

Ledra Brady, who was the clerk for the D.C. intelligence squad, was considered Shoffler's closest confidant there. When asked if she knew why Shoffler was outside the Watergate that night, she said "There are no coincidences." Beyond that, apparently, she was unwilling to go. "There are some things Carl and I will just keep to ourselves," she said in a 2012 phone interview. "I will tell you this, though. Carl was a very honorable man."

After leaving the D.C. police, Ledra reportedly took a job for the Drug Enforcement Administration in Mexico. There are those who believe that the DEA assignment was a cover for work she was doing for the CIA. She has not responded to calls asking her to comment on those suspicions.

[98] Rothstein, who spoke with the author in 2013, says he first encountered Shoffler in the early 70s, in the course of a nationwide pedophile investigation in which they were both involved. At first, he says, they only exchanged information over the phone. About 1977, however, they met face-to-face when Rothstein attended a meeting of intelligence officers at the Washington Navy Yard, in Washington, D.C.

It was shortly thereafter, he says, that Shoffler told him that he had known in advance about the Watergate burglary. However, when Rothstein asked him who tipped him off, Shoffler would only say, "It was the one who got religion." Rothstein believes that would be Watergate wireman James McCord, who wrote a strange, almost indecipherable Watergate book entitled *A Piece of Tape*, full of apocalyptic Biblical references and prophesies.

[99] *Secret Agenda*, p. 321.

[100] "June 17, 1972. Nine o'clock Saturday morning. Early for the telephone. Woodward fumbled for the receiver and snapped awake. The city editor of the *Washington Post* was

on the line. Five men had been arrested earlier that morning in a burglary at Democratic headquarters, carrying photographic equipment and electronic gear. Could he come in?" Opening paragraph of *All the President's Men* (1975) by Carl Bernstein and Bob Woodward.

[101] An initial amount of $220,000 was raised by longtime campaign moneyman Herbert Kalmbach. As Rosen writes in *Strong Man* (p. 317), when Kalmbach got cold feet, "Dean would have to find a new source for the burglar's hush money." After that Dean started dipping into a White House slush fund of about $350,000 (p. 339).

[102] Russell's bank records, obtained by Liddy's lawyer John B. Williams, reveal that Russell's account balances rarely exceeded a few hundred dollars. On Nov. 15, 1972, however—shortly after Dean withdrew $4,850 from a White House safe—Russell deposited $4,570 in his account. Dean would later tell Senate investigators he used the funds for his honeymoon, and subsequently paid them back. Questioned by Williams, however, he was unable to give an adequate accounting of how he spent the money.

Bank records show that in March 1973, Russell deposited another $20,895 in his account. This was about the same time Dean is alleged to have taken another $22,000 from White House Funds. In his 1976 book Ends of Power, former White House chief of staff H.R. Haldeman reported that he attempted to trace the missing money and ultimately concluded that Dean took the $22,000 and never returned it.

[103] In the forward to his 2006 book *Conservatives Without Conscience,* Dean dismisses Bailley as a nut whose word cannot be taken seriously. "When we deposed him," Dean writes, "Bailley's attorney arranged for a psychiatrist to testify under oath that his client's mental condition made him unable to distinguish fact from fiction." Recent interviews with Bailley's long-time lawyer, Richard Murray, and with Dr. Tony Tsitos, Bailley's therapist at the time of the depositions, prove this to be false.

Murray says he never suggested, and furthermore, never thought, that Bailley was unable to distinguish fact from fiction. He says he tried to get Bailley excused from having to be deposed because Bailley was taking medicine, prescribed by Bailley's therapist at the time. Over the course of his relationship with Bailley, he says, he has "never thought that Bailley was telling anything but the truth. In fact, I'm quite convinced he is."

Dean further attempts to dismiss Bailley by saying he has been "in and out of mental institutions throughout his adult life." Considering the evidence that Dean himself may have been involved in having Bailley wrongfully committed to St. Elizabeth's, this is more than a little disingenuous. Bailley, who suffers from post-traumatic stress—caused, it should noted, by the shock of being thrown into ward for the criminally insane at St. Elizabeth's and then prison—says he has been hospitalized twice. Once after witnessing a murder in Seattle, and then again several years later, after watching the 911 attacks on T.V.

Dr. Tsitos is also quite emphatic: "I was never deposed. I was never approached to be deposed. If I had testified, I would never have said Phil Bailey couldn't tell fact from fiction. It's just not so."

[104] For the guest list, see *Mo,* p. 63.

[105] "Old Gambler Mourns Days of $20,000 roll," *Washington Post,* Dec. 23, 1972.

[106] See for example, the *Harvard Crimson,* Apr. 15, 1974: "Hoffa has formed a new prison reform organization called the National Association for Justice since his release in December 1971, and he has been traveling around the country promoting it." If those student journalists could figure this out, presumably Woodward could too.

[107] "In his new position [as communications duty officer for the Chief of Naval Operations], Woodward presided over all communications traffic going to and from the CNO's office. This included top-secret communiqués from the White House, the CIA, the National Security Agency (NSA), the State Department, the Defense Intelligence Agency (DIA) and the NSC . . . He held, in other words, a position of strategic trust within the intelligence community." *Secret Agenda,* p. 294.

[108] "Pentagon Got Secret Data of Kissinger's" by Bob Woodward and Carl Bernstein, *Washington Post,* Jan. 12, 1974. For Colodny's comment on this article, see *The Forty Years War,* p. 211–12: "The article . . . took the Haig-Buzhardt-Moorer line—that the espionage had done no harm and that the whole thing was [Yeoman Charles] Radford's fault. Nor did the article disclose Woodward's prior relationship to Welander, an omission that constituted a violation of professional ethics." See *Silent Coup f*or the best account of the military spy ring and its crucial role in the Watergate affair.

[109] "Memorandum for the Deputy Director for Plans by Eric Eisenstadt," Mar. 1, 1973, from the Nedzi Report: *Inquiry Into Alleged Involvement of the CIA in Watergate,* House Armed Services Committee, 94th Congress, pp. 1073–76.

Hougan quotes the memo in full in *Secret Agenda,* pp. 332–35: "Mr. Bennett said also that he has been feeding stories to Bob Woodward of the *Washington Post* with the understanding that there will be no attribution to Bennett. Woodward is suitably grateful for the fine stories and by-lines which he gets and protects Bennett (and the Mullen Company)." The Mullen Company, of course, was the CIA front that employed Howard Hunt after his supposed retirement from the Agency.

[110] The book was *Yours in Truth* (2012) by Jeff Himmelman. For Himmelman's response to Woodward, who called the book "dishonest," see "The Storm Over My Ben Bradlee Book," online at thedailybeast.com/articles/2012/05/05.

[111] Buried in a long article, "Mystery Solved," *New York Times,* June 2, 2005, written on the occasion of Woodard's supposed outing of former FBI official Mark Felt as Deep Throat:

"David Obst, the former literary agent for Mr. Woodward and Mr. Bernstein, has long contended that Deep Throat was actually a composite of several anonymous sources—a view he still held after Tuesday's disclosures.

"'Mark Felt was an invaluable source to the *Washington Post* and to Woodward and Bernstein, but he was not Deep Throat—there was no Deep Throat,' said Mr. Obst, who claims that the character was added to the original draft of *All the President's Men* to give it more intrigue."

[112] As Rosen writes in *The Strong Man*, a 1974 internal memorandum by George Frampton of the Watergate Special Prosecutors Force "noted 'significant discrepancies between Dean's anticipated trial testimony [and] that of other Government witnesses or evidence.' Another internal WSPF memorandum, prepared in February 1974 and also previously unpublished, demolished the myth, promulgated by Senator Ervin, among others, that Dean's testimony before the Senate Watergate committee was 'corroborated in all significant respects by the taped recordings' of President Nixon. The WSPF memo bore the title 'Material Discrepancies Between the Senate Select Committee Testimony of John Dean and the Tapes of Dean's Meetings with the President.'" *Strong Man,* pp. 320.

[113] The presence of Weicker's name and contact information in Heidi's little black book can perhaps be easily explained. He was, after all, a friend and neighbor of the Deans. Not so easy to explain, however, is the entry in Heidi's book for Sam Dash, chief counsel for the Watergate committee. Yet, unmistakably, Dash's home address and unlisted phone number are in it.

Entries in Heidi's little black book for U.S. Senator Lowell Weicker and Watergate Special Committee counsel Sam Dash.

[114] For books on Lyndon Johnson's transgressions, see *A Texan Looks at Lyndon* (1964) by J. Evetts Haley. Also *LBJ, Mastermind of the JFK Assassination* (2011) by Phillip F. Nelson. Regardless of what one may think about Nelson's assassination theories, the book provides an excellent summary of LBJ's history of corruption. See also "The Killing of Henry Marshall" by Bill Adler, *The Texas Observer*, Nov. 7, 1986.

[115] *Maureen K. Dean and John W. Dean v. St. Martins Press, Inc., et al.,* Civil Action No. 91-1807.

In addition to Colodny and Gettlin, who wrote *Silent Coup,* and St. Martins Press, which published it, the Deans sued more than a hundred others, including this author, charging them with defamation. Like most of the others, I was dismissed from the lawsuit soon after it was filed.

As Hougan, who was also dropped from the lawsuit, writes: "For his part, Liddy refused to back down, wishing to take the case to court so that he could get Dean on the witness stand. In that, Liddy was unsuccessful. The case against him was dismissed." See Hougan's essay, "Hougan, Liddy, the Post and Watergate" on his website jimhougan.com/wordpress.

[116] "In fact, according to a little-noticed Sept. 27, 1999 judge's order, Dean dropped his suit against Colodny. The author (and the judge) accepted the deal only on condition that the former White House lawyer promise never to sue him for defamation again. Colodny's insurance company also paid him $410,000 to make the suit go away."

Jeff Stein, "Watergate Bugging—again," *AND Magazine*, July 16, 2013.

[117] *Ida Maxwell Wells v. G. Gordon Liddy,* Civil Action No. JFM-97-946. Second lawsuit: *Wells v. Liddy*, Civil No. JFM-97-946. Maxie Wells's case certainly wasn't helped when a letter she wrote to a friend, shortly after the Watergate arrests, was placed in evidence. "It appears," she wrote, "that the Republicans are going to try to discredit Demo witnesses on moral grounds. They've got the makings of a good scandal in my case . . . I shouldn't write, but must confide in someone." The letter, entered as an exhibit in *Wells v. Liddy,* has also been reproduced in Liddy's book, *When I Was a Kid, This Was a Free Country,* pp. 197–98.

[118] *Washington Post*, Feb. 4, 2001.

[119] In the spring of 1973, just as Dean was preparing to jump to the prosecution, Dean asked Mo's old friend Jack Garfield to take Mo and Heidi to stay for a while at the Palm Bay Club in Miami, where his old prep school friend, Lance Cooper, was the golf pro. Mo mentions this trip in her book, but doesn't mention Heidi. She also fails to mention that Cooper—"*Dear* Lance," as she calls him—was not just a golf pro, but a big time bookie and social arranger for the Palm Bay Club set.

In 1976, Cooper would be indicted on felony charges of bookmaking and keeping a gambling house. He was convicted, fined $1,500 and placed on two years probation.

Happily, it was determined that no members of the Dolphins had been involved in Cooper's gambling enterprises. Associated Press story in the *Ocala-Star Banner,* May 6, 1977.

As Garfield could not fail to notice, Cooper was always surrounded by a bevy of good-looking young women, and was clearly in the match-making business. In recent interviews, Garfield described him as "sort of pimpish." In fact, says Garfield, in the mid-'70s Cooper sent him a young woman, who had been part of the party scene at the Palm Bay Club. The woman, who will not be identified here, lived at Garfield's house in Bel Air for several months before finding a suitably wealthy boyfriend. She is now married and living a respectable life in Beverly Hills.

[120] "John W. Dean The Third?" by Maxine Cheshire, *Washington Post,* July 3, 1973.

[121] Thanks to my friend Dave Wagner for the succinct characterization of Mo's *Washington Wives.*

Jack Garfield and Mo in D.C., 1973.

APPENDIX

The McGowan Affidavit

Statement of David McGowan

1. My name is David McGowan. I reside at 4400 East West Highway in Bethesda, Maryland.

2. During the late 1960s and through mid 1970, I was acquainted with a woman named Heidi Rikan. Heidi was a very beautiful woman who lived in an apartment building on River Road in Bethesda, Maryland. Heidi had a reputation as a prostitute. She would frequent bars and nightclubs in Washington, D.C., and would engage in sexual acts with men in exchange for money. I was one of those men. On two or three occasions during this time, I met Heidi at a bar and we subsequently engaged in sexual intercourse, after which I paid her an amount of money in exchange. I recall having sex with Heidi at her River Road apartment and at my residence on Quaker Lane in Alexandria, Virginia. I recall paying her approximately $ 50 for each occasion.

3. During this period of time, I also became acquainted with Maureen Biner, who subsequently became Maureen Dean. Heidi Rikan brought Maureen to meet Richie McCaleb at the Quaker Lane home rented by Richie. Richie and Maureen had sex the first time they met. Subsequently, I learned from Richie that Maureen was "broke" and "looking for a sponsor." Maureen visited the Quaker Lane home a number of times, always having sexual intercourse with Richie. Sometimes the door to Richie's bedroom would be left open, and I could see them having sex as I passed by on the way to my bedroom. Maureen would observe me, and appear not to care. I also observed one or two hundred dollar bills on the dresser in Richie's room when Maureen would visit, which was unusual because that is not where Richie kept his money. When Maureen left, the money was gone.

4. Both Heidi and Maureen had reputations as party girls who would engage in sex for money. I was told by Billy Rice, now deceased, that he had paid both Heidi and Maureen for sex.

Dated: 3-31-96

David A McGowan
David McGowan

David McGowan, who gave this affidavit to defense attorney John Williams in the course of the Dean v. St. Martins *case, was a D.C. bookie and part of Joe Nesline's football gambling operation. His colleague and roommate, Richie McCaleb, who figures prominently in the affidavit, is listed in Heidi's little black book.*

In 1968, both McGowan and McCaleb were indicted in federal court for running a "football gambling pool" that apparently involved several members of the Washington Redskins. See Endnote 19 on page 157.

In her Aug. 28, 1966 deposition in the St. Martins case, Mo Dean, not too surprisingly, testified that she never met Richie McCaleb.

INDEX

Note: Entries in this index vary from page to sentence-level entries. Book titles and illustrations (photographs, documents) are denoted by *italics*. Persons with multiple surnames are listed in main entry under the most commonly used surname.

PHOTO CREDITS